MW00564266

READ THIS

and

CALL ME IN THE MORNING

a prescription for teen substance
use prevention *with cartoons*

FIONA BROWN, LPC, M.Ed./Ed.S.

Read This and Call Me in The Morning:
A prescription for teen substance use prevention,
First Edition

© 2023 Fiona Brown, LPC

All rights reserved.

Published by BookBaby

7905 North Route 130 • Pennsauken, NJ 08110

Written and illustrated by Fiona Brown, LPC, M.Ed./Ed.S.

Print ISBN: 978-1-66788-724-1
eBook ISBN: 978-1-66788-725-8

Disclaimer Notice: The content in this book is intended for informational purposes only and is not a replacement for medical advice. Only a medical or mental health professional can give you tailored, personalized medical, mental or behavioral health recommendations according to your specific needs.

This book is dedicated to the parents who trusted me with their children and to their children who trusted me with their stories.

And to my husband and children who put up with late nights, multi-tasking and the never-ending "almost done." I love you googolplex.

To my friends and colleagues, thank you for keeping a straight face and encouraging my foolish dream in true therapist fashion.

Dear parents of a perfect kid,

The wish list we have for our children grows longer every day. Your list, like mine, might include wishes that they'll be well-liked, act with kindness, be honest, find hobbies they love and do well in school. And like me you no doubt want them to succeed in all things and be happy with the life you've made for them and that they make for themselves.

It would be comforting to believe that if our children embody all the beauty and talent that we can imagine for them they couldn't also get drawn into unhealthy behaviors and their inherent consequences. But this is the lie we tell ourselves - that our bright, beautiful, perfect children couldn't possibly engage in problematic, self-destructive behavior like substance abuse.

It didn't take long working in the field of substance abuse treatment to discover how dangerous this thought process can be. Taking for granted that we know who will and won't make it out of teenage experimentation is risky because it's based primarily on stereotypes about the type of people who become addicted. The truth is that addiction affects people across all age, gender, race, ethnicity and socio-economic groups. Changes in the brain caused by substance use will happen to anyone who uses regularly and heavily enough.

I have met perfect kids over and over again. They are likable, talented and brilliant and are brought to my office by bewildered, adoring parents. In most cases they have been second-chanced almost to death by people who gen- uinely care about them and believe in the eventuality that they will figure it out. As their friends and loved ones unintentionally enable them, the drug wreaks havoc in their brain until their addiction rages, gradually tearing everything away from them.

The truth is that even the most wonderful people are changed by using. As the weeks, months and years stretch on, they find themselves in darker places doing things that starkly contrast who they are. And then the stereotypes of a selfish, unmotivated, dangerous (etc.) addict start to fit and those stereotypes are strengthened, regardless of who that person was before they started using.

Substance use requires time and lack of intervention to grow and what better opportunity than a young person who seemingly has it all? If the conditions in a person's brain (i.e. genetic predisposition or mental illness) and in their environment (i.e. traumatic events, enabling) are ripe for substance use, then their relative success in school, hobbies or other areas might not be enough to keep them healthy.

Our perfect kids need us to remain open to the possibility that the bumps along the way could be fueling or fueled by substance use. By doing so we can address the real problem at hand and avoid letting it escalate unchecked. Considering the possibility that our beautiful, smart, talented children could be using doesn't diminish any of these truths about them. And having open eyes doesn't make us any less loving and supportive. Society has seen countless talented, kind, deeply loved people suffer through addiction, so why do we still assume that people who possess these traits cannot be affected by this deadly disease?

The more you learn about the disease of addiction I know you will find, like I have, that people can be wonderful and still fall down the slippery slope of drug use or addiction. Perfect kids and perfectly imperfect parents do not get a free pass.

My teenage clients consistently describe their period of heaviest use as being in a fog they didn't realize they were in. I promise you; this is a fog that anyone, even your perfect kid, can get lost in. So, if you have a perfect kid like so many of us do, keep reading - this book is for you, for me, for all of us.

TABLE OF CONTENTS

PART IV: WAIVE THE RED FLAG

PART V: FINAL THOUGHTS

chapter one

FREQUENTLY ASKED QUESTIONS

FREQUENTLY ASKED QUESTIONS ARE THE ORIGINAL life hack. A wealth of information thoughtfully assembled by a gatekeeper of the details we can all benefit from. I love FAQ lists and often navigate my way to this page on a website to discover which answers I never knew I needed. Because let's face it, sometimes you just don't know what you don't know.

Throughout my career I have worked in a few different counseling offices serving teens and their families. On many occasions as I walked through the lobby and looked at the variety of information-giving signs, I wondered what it would be like to create an FAQ poster for therapy. It became somewhat of a game to imagine the questions and answers we might post.

For teens and their families visiting the office to see me - a specialist in substance abuse assessment and treatment - the questions might include, "How do I talk to my child about drugs?", "Is this really a big deal?" or "Why won't they just stop?" And as I pondered the most common questions I encountered; I enjoyed the absurdity of trying to fit the answers to them on a 24" x 36" poster. But I always thought they might fit in a book…

Every young person, and therefore every parent, deals with this issue in one way or another. Just like bullying, heartbreak and conflict are challenging parts of life, so too are the decisions we make around substance use. As parents, we can leverage the power of our relationship to help our children make those decisions armed with accurate information and critical thinking skills.

Although each teen and family is unique, the "need to know" information that allows parents to have healthy conversations and respond effectively to substance use is universal. As a result, substance abuse prevention and treatment specialists like myself repeatedly share the same baseline concepts with young people and their families so they can make sense of this problem and find healthy ways to move forward.

I have spent countless hours on phone calls and in therapy sessions with parents who feel like deer in headlights grappling with the discovery of their child's drug use. I love my work and I love helping parents get caught up to speed on this issue, but I admit I wished there was an easier way. I've long fantasized about handing parents a book, saying "Read this and call me in the morning" to expedite the process. After a decade of wishing I could provide a resource like this but not finding anything to fit, I decided I should quit my whining and write one.

What we do as therapists is scientific, especially as substance abuse treatment specialists. And while we nerd out on the latest research findings and developments in neuroscience, having such a deep academic understanding is not essential for parents to successfully address this issue with their children. I mean, who wants to go wading through dense research articles, scouring the depths of universities and public health organizations?

Me, that's who! Allow me to spare you the time and energy by translating and summarizing substance use prevention information into the basics that will help you parent effectively.

Parents wear many hats: chef, doctor, chauffeur, stylist, among others, but we don't need to add 'substance use expert' to that list. It is, however, helpful for you to "get it" just enough so that you are able to engage with your kids and identify this issue early on. They say there are no shortcuts in life, but I disagree. This book is exactly that, a shortcut to "getting it". What follows will focus on the fundamentals that every parent needs to successfully:

Identify risk factors for teen substance use and how to protect against them

- *Understand how substance abuse affects the developing teen brain*
- *Understand the interaction between substance use and mental health*
- *Have healthy, direct conversations with your child*
- *Identify and respond to early warning signs of substance use*

chapter two

THIS (MIGHT BE) A DRILL

A FRIEND AND COLLEAGUE, BLAISE, LIKES TO SAY THAT we talk about substance use early for the same reason we practice fire drills; not because there is a fire and not because we know there will be a fire, but because there might be one in the future. I love this analogy because it highlights the importance of thoughtfully preparing ourselves regardless of whether we believe it is likely to happen in our family.

The perfect time to address substance use is before it causes serious consequences, before it wreaks havoc on relationships, before it has a chance to change the course of someone's life. Talking early and often and giving our kids a safe space to turn when this issue arises might be all it takes to head this off at the pass.

The best case scenario is that substance use is a tiny blip on your radar or no blip at all. For most it is understandably difficult to imagine that this could ever be an issue for their family. And one day I hope you look back and wonder why you spent your time reading this book and having these conversations with your children. Effective prevention means that we never see the things that don't happen. We never know what could have been on the other side had we not taken early action.

I don't fault parents for wanting to ignore or avoid this topic until it smacks them in the face. Substance use is not only scary but somewhat bewildering as well. It would be nice if we could close our eyes to this issue and hope for the best, but avoidance won't do us any favors.

We teach our kids about dental hygiene, knowing that we are preventing cavities by equipping them with this knowledge and skill. We incorporate healthy foods in their diet so they can grow to their potential. We get them involved in sports and encourage physical activity so they can lead a healthy, active lifestyle. We can feel just as confident that by preparing our kids for situations where alcohol and drugs are available or helping them connect their use to changes in their overall well-being, we are reducing risk and possibly averting a serious health problem.

According to the Substance Abuse and Mental Health Services Administration (SAMHSA), "It is never too early to talk to your children about alcohol and other drugs. Children as young as nine years old already start viewing alcohol in a more positive way, and approximately 3,300 kids as young as 12 try marijuana each day."[1] As I write this my son is nearing that 12-year-old mark and if I hadn't met so many teens who reported age 12 as their age of first marijuana use, I would absolutely not believe it to be possible. I am grateful that my experience as a therapist has shed light on the realities of teen life and yet this is still an upsetting possibility to consider for the perfect kid I love so deeply.

What brings me comfort as I walk into this season of life with him is the knowledge I have about how I can prepare him and be a solid source of support. This knowledge is based on nearly two decades of education, training and experience working with teens and their families. I hope that by sharing this information with you here, you will also feel a sense of confidence in your ability to face this issue head on.

We as parents are in the best possible position to be preventative. We watch our children's every move, know them like no one else and form the strongest of connections with them. What we say and do is truly meaningful and impactful. Although our children are likely to receive information about substance use in schools or other settings, the most important place for these conversations to happen is in the home.

chapter three

WHAT'S WITH THE CARTOONS?

WHEN I BEGAN MY CAREER IN SUBSTANCE USE TREAT-ment, I met with groups of 10 or so teens with substance use disorders for 90 minutes, twice a week. And let me tell you, they were a tough crowd. From all walks of life - gang members to prep school athletes - they almost always arrived stone-faced and resistant to engage in any way.

At first, I assumed their resistance meant a lack of willingness to change. But within a few months, it became apparent that their attitude toward treatment was much more about their expectation of me and the experience itself than about whether or not they wanted to improve their lives. These teens expected me to lecture and judge them as so many adults in their lives already had. They shared stories about adults embarrassing them in front of peers, calling them names, shaming them and even being verbally and physically abusive.

I imagine that the adults in their lives were hoping to scare them straight, get them to see the light or some other ineffective cliche. But this bad behavior on the part of trusted adults and authority figures had the opposite of the intended effect. As bad behavior tends to do, these confrontations caused teens to focus more on the aggressor's behavior and less on their own. Feeling shamed and disrespected led them to discount the advice and guidance they received from these adults despite its accuracy.

What was missing from these unsuccessful interactions was connection. One of the first lessons we learn as therapists is to connect with people before delivering content. This is important for therapists and parents alike because a person will value the ideas and information you have to share only if they feel a connection to you. If you don't have a connection, your content won't be received. Well-meaning adults were trying desperately to effect some change with accurate information (aka content) but undermined any connection with harmful words and actions, leaving everyone frustrated and exhausted from these unsuccessful interactions.

I decided I would try to provide such a different experience of treatment than was expected that I would essentially confuse these teens into unintentional participation. Part therapist, part stand-up comedian, I found creative ways to engage them. We sat on the floor to get out of our comfort zone and shift our perspective. We tried yoga and mindfulness. We colored and had puppet shows. And since I had a large whiteboard, I would create crude illustrations as I talked about certain topics or even as group members talked to help make connections to what they were sharing.

By some miracle, my silly cartoons resonated with them. These drawings lightened the mood, helped them make sense of the information and became an interactive way to convey their own experience. Seeing the information in black and white changed the way we talked about the emotionally-laden topics of drug use and mental health. Pictures are objective and honest and they don't judge, especially when they're poorly drawn.

These cartoons have been valuable to me in helping teens understand some essential concepts about substance use and addiction. They also serve as a tangible representation of the changes happening in their brain that they feel but aren't able to put their finger on. So, when I finally sat down to put this book together, I thought the cartoons might help you, too. And, like every successful college graduate, I seized an opportunity to increase my page count without working too hard.

Cartoons help me stay grounded in my work with teens. They remind me that talking isn't always the best way to connect. They keep me from taking myself too seriously and help me focus more on my connection with the person across from me. Finally, cartoons help set the tone for my meetings with teens, encouraging vulnerability and allowing humor to creep into these often-intimidating conversations.

Cartoons evolved to become part of my approach that works for me, but that isn't right for everyone. For you, these conversations might be best tackled over a shared interest like puzzles, while watching trash tv or taking a walk- the possibilities are endless! Authenticity is critical so finding what works for you and your child that feels comfortable and honest is most important. But if you're feeling stuck or unsure, consider it my clinical recommendation to embarrass yourself deeply with stick-figure cartoons to get the ball rolling.

chapter four

CHECKING YOUR BIAS

IN THE UNITED STATES, WE HAVE PLACED A GREATER emphasis on the topic of mental health and normalizing mental health care in recent years. Prominent public figures are sharing honestly about their own struggles with mental illness and encouraging help-seeking. Mainstream media highlights advances in mental health research and care and promotes a holistic view of our well-being. Social media influencers are getting in on the wave as well and now a new genre of social media content dishes out advice and advocates for healthy behaviors and help-seeking.

We are undoubtedly facing a teen mental health crisis in the United States, but I challenge us to stay focused on what we're doing right. Teenage rates of depression have increased due to a variety of factors but thank goodness stigma and codes of silence are less and less a part of this picture. Paving the way for dialogue about mental health struggles is something we should be proud of and these changes to our cultural attitudes are having a positive impact on our kids.

Growing up in a society more open and honest about mental health and mental illness has increasingly encouraged children to prioritize their well-being and talk about these issues. Now more than ever they are connecting to their own thoughts and feelings and seeking help for themselves and their peers. This budding acceptance of mental health and mental illness is a welcome change and is a step toward a healthier society as a whole. While I celebrate this success, I think it begs the question, "why should substance use be any different?"

Most people I meet have an awareness of the seriousness of substance use and want more prevention and treatment to address this issue. This tends to change, though, when it comes to talking to their child or providing education in their community. The message consistently sent by this avoidance and discomfort is that using drugs is a bad thing that bad people do and if we talk about it, we're going to encourage people to use or make it worse.

Like other mental health issues, substance use dramatically affects our social-emotional well-being and has implications for our overall health. Do we judge it differently because it is a chosen behavior? Many serious illnesses like obesity, heart disease and lung cancer result from chosen lifestyles and behavior. Or might it be because we view drug use as a moral/values issue? Suicide is also viewed from some religious perspectives as a violation of their values, yet we have managed to understand suicide risk as worthy of our efforts and attention.

If I may just stand here on my soapbox for a moment, I believe our discomfort with this topic is rooted in the bias we have toward people who use alcohol and other drugs. Despite the fact that substance use affects people from across all gender, racial, ethnic and socioeconomic backgrounds, we still expect that people with substance use problems fit a certain undesirable mold.

Our brain loves to categorize things into **schema**, which are shorthand ways to understand the world and fit things into cognitive boxes. When we come across something we aren't familiar with, we make sense of it using the schema we have about how the world works. Our lived experiences and the information we receive from our environment help create these schemas. Given the limitations of our own lived experiences within our corner of the world, it is only natural that our schemas are created with bias.

If a child's personality or other characteristics don't seem to fit our schema for a person at risk for or affected by substance use, then it is easy to dismiss any evidence indicating that this could be a problem for them. This schema, while intended to help us make sense of things, does little to no good when it comes to early substance use. Young people just beginning to exhibit symptoms of problematic use, when early intervention is most critical, are not the disheveled, out of control, desperate image most often painted of someone with a drug problem.

I've had many, many conversations with parents who adamantly deny clear warning signs of substance use because they don't view their child as fitting their preconceived notions of someone with a drug problem. And God forbid someone like me accuses their child of having a problem with substance use. Despite my credentials and experience, it is near-impossible to convince these parents that accusing someone of problematic drug use is like accusing someone of having diabetes.

With the understandable hope that their child could be having any problem other than substance use, parents look far and wide in every other possible direction. By doing so, they manage to convince themselves of some alternative explanation. And when they see other teens or adults with severe addiction symptoms whose attitudes, behaviors or appearance fit their narrow idea of drug use, **confirmation bias** reinforces their belief that they know exactly what and who drug use looks like.

When parents are focused on the wrong explanation, they spend precious time and energy on solutions that won't work because they're not designed to address this issue. The best medicines, doctor visits, therapy, mentoring, tutoring or academic interventions ultimately won't work because substance using pegs don't fit into academic, medical or mental health holes.

Parents aren't the only ones whose efforts can be derailed by bias when interpreting symptoms. Anyone who interacts with these children and who does not have the experience to recognize signs and symptoms of substance use is likely to draw a conclusion they are more familiar or comfortable with. They, too, will expend time and effort on misguided solutions that ultimately bear no fruit.

This is frustrating and exhausting for all involved and can lead to conflict among parents, school and community members and care providers as each system assumes another is failing the child when no progress is made. As parents and professionals look the other way, the teen continues to use and convinces themselves that using isn't the problem because adults have done a great job of providing alternative explanations. By avoiding the real issue, the teen's symptoms continue to get worse.

I know this may sound like a very specific unfolding of events or something that only happens under rare conditions, but I assure you it is not. This, from my perspective, is actually very common and predictable because of our bias about what drug use looks like and the resulting resistance to acknowledge this issue.

There are a number of legitimate challenges a child may be facing including medical conditions, environmental stressors, mental illnesses or learning disabilities, among others. Investing in support and treatment to address these concerns is vital but we need to account for any substance use when we evaluate someone's needs. Substance abuse is a brain health issue which seriously impacts a variety of cognitive, emotional and behavioral processes that affect one another. This makes it very difficult to accurately diagnose another condition until or unless the person is drug-free.

To avoid letting our bias get in the way, we should routinely and regularly rule out substance use with an objective source before pursuing any other diagnoses or treatments for teens. Ruling out substance use as a standard first step in assessing someone's overall health can take stigma out of this process, keeping the focus where it belongs - on health and well-being. Getting an accurate picture early on will also save families a great deal of time, money and emotional energy. Most importantly, they will get the answers they need to help their teens lead their best lives. We will get more detailed about ruling out substance use in Chapter 26 titled (what else?) Ruling it out.

chapter five

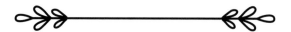

FEAR NOT

APPROACHING THIS TOPIC MAY FEEL LIKE PREPARING for a tightrope walk when parenting already feels very much like one. Teen substance use is scary. Lives are altered and lost and the shame and stigma associated with unmanageable dependency prevents far too many from seeking help. But, as we will explore further, the way forward is not with shocking statistics or scare tactics. The way forward is with awareness and understanding of this health issue so we can engage in healthy dialogue, make healthy decisions and seek appropriate health care when we need it.

Let's make a deal: I promise not to use scare tactics with you if you promise not to use them with your kids. I know that warnings and dramatic stories might make you feel like you are instilling a healthy sense of fear in your children, but feelings are not facts. Despite how we might feel when delivering these messages, they are not sufficient in protecting our children from the risks of substance use.

Fear-based messaging became a popular tool in substance use prevention in the 1960s in response to the popularization of the drug culture during this era. Since then perspectives on whether or not this is effective have varied. A review of the available research on fear-based messaging specific to youth substance use prevention was conducted in 2014 by the Substance Abuse and Mental Health Services Administration. This study revealed that **scare tactics** are especially ineffective when applied to youth substance use prevention efforts.[2] My less-scientific perspective based on working with teens leads me to agree with this conclusion.

Almost every young person I've encountered in drug treatment has said that they were afraid of alcohol and other drugs when they were young. Some had even made commitments never to use drugs. As they got older they were confronted with very different information. They heard from friends and news media that vaping and marijuana use are "healthier," "safer" or "medicinal". They experimented themselves and saw other people experimenting without dire consequences. This discrepancy between ominous warnings and their lived experiences eroded that fear away and introduced skepticism about the validity of warnings made by adults in general and parents in particular.

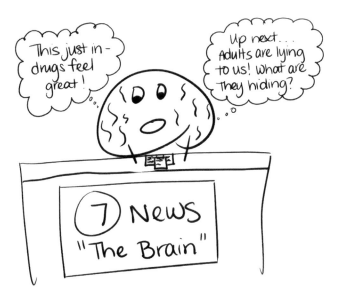

Even if fear-based messages might have some initial impact on younger kids, they can't be the single strategy employed to deter people from a particular behavior. We can't solely rely on emotionally laden messages in an attempt to control our children's behavior. Preparing people with actual skills they need to make informed choices will take them farther.

In the United States in particular, we've been beating our heads against this same wall of scare tactics for decades and have only succeeded in creating a stigmatizing and silencing culture around drug use. The hush-hush attitude about drug use makes it seem mysterious and therefore alluring for some. For others it can lead to ignorance about the realities of problematic use and fear about seeking information. Fear of stigma also serves to cut off opportunities for prevention and early intervention for those who become involved in drug use.

Earlier today I was talking to a student about joining a recovery group at school. Despite her pride in herself and her success being sober, she was afraid of others seeing her in the group and knowing she was in recovery. Revealing she was in recovery meant that she once had a problem with drug use. This is a sad reminder of the stigma that continues to surround this issue - that people are reluctant to even celebrate their success because it would reveal something they believe they should be ashamed of.

We will be ditching the scare tactics and stigma and focusing on using a straightforward, health-driven and conversational approach. We will make space for honesty and open discussion about substance use. This will give our kids opportunity and permission to ask questions and share details that will protect them. Through these interactions, our children will build critical thinking skills and even develop plans for risky situations that will serve them well when they face these real-life choice points without us.

Maintaining an easygoing, non-judgmental tone is the cornerstone of my work in both treatment and prevention with teens. Easy to say as a therapist, right? Therapists are expected to be unbiased and objective so no surprise there. But as a parent? Nonjudgmental? Not exactly an easy task, but I promise you it's possible. We can set limits, impart wisdom and give factual warnings about drug use while maintaining a non-judgmental view of the person making decisions.

Encouraging open discussion and avoiding fearmongering does NOT mean we are giving people the green light to dive headfirst into drug use. Nor does it mean we will be sending the message that drug use is acceptable in any way. This shift does not require us to become more permissive, it requires us to become more intentional with our messaging and more accurate with our information. We will be focusing on factual information, not on emotionally charged messages. Our ultimate goal is to be a safe, consistent, trustworthy source of information and guidance and we are going to do so without drama. We will be covering the specifics of how to go about having these conversations in Part IV.

Our first step in preparing ourselves to be unbiased and nonjudgmental about people with problematic substance use is to gain an appreciation for the reasons teens use in the first place.

A NOTE ABOUT FENTANYL:

Fentanyl has been making headlines recently due to its high potency and lethality, even in trace amounts. Although we are focusing on reducing our use of scare tactics, factual warnings about Fentanyl are legitimately scary. Fentanyl is a synthetic opioid (pain-blocker) that is 50-100 times stronger than morphine. It is used in extreme circumstances to treat severe pain under medical supervision. Due to low manufacturing cost, illicit drugs may be laced with fentanyl to increase the intensity of the high. Teens should be aware of the risk of pills and other drugs being laced with fentanyl and the very real potential for overdose. The Drug Enforcement Administration's website offers information for parents and tips for discussing fentanyl with teens.[3] Here are a few tips for talking to teens about fentanyl:

1. Explain what fentanyl is and that it's high potency makes it extremely dangerous even for one-time use.

2. Explain that fentanyl has been detected in nearly every type of drug (marijuana, cocaine, pills, etc.) and is not detectable to the naked eye.

3. Explain that purchasing any kind of drug from an unregulated source (i.e., drug dealer) means risking unintentional use of fentanyl.

chapter six

UNDER THE INFLUENCE
(WHY TEENS USE)

MOST OF US CAN SAY THAT AT SOME POINT WE HAVE been the willing victims of a social media influencer. If you are unfamiliar, an influencer is someone with a social media account who shows us how much better we can be if we just look like them, act like them and get things for free in exchange for advertising.

I have had more conversations than I care to admit with my sons about the YouTube videos of Lamborghinis, mansions and giveaways that are clearly rented, leased and staged. Yet despite my very obvious social media prowess as a 38-year-old mom of two, my children refuse to believe me. These narratives, perpetuated by popular storytellers, are hard to dismiss. Appearances are incredibly real to young people who are so drawn in by the confidence of others.

If alcohol and drugs were social media influencers, they would appear to be living the dream. We would scroll through their feeds and see carefully selected images of exciting and care-free adventures with friends. We would read philosophical captions about what they believe they've learned about life and themselves. We would see the promise of a life without mental illness, fear of failure or the stressors of reality. We would see on full display the bait laid out by alcohol and drugs of a promised lifestyle of fun and freedom from our unloved selves.

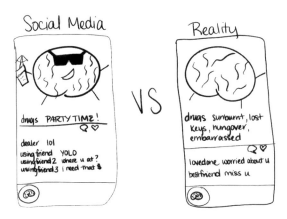

Alcohol and drug use is a lifestyle. It involves the people, places and things that make up the culture of using. And we cannot deny that the lifestyle found in alcohol and drugs is at first what was promised. It numbs pain, quells anxiety, erases bad memories, forgets stress, restores courage, manufactures connections and helps you fit in. The fact that these things ultimately lead to disaster seems an unlikely problem for future us.

Before we as parents can preach about risks and consequences, we must acknowledge the drug and alcohol lifestyle's carefully curated highlight reel and the early days when it delivers on its promise. It is from this place of acknowledging what is that we can begin chipping away at the realities of where that path leads. Uncomfortable though this acknowledgment may be, let's explore the very real attractions of the drug use lifestyle that we must reckon with.

People use drugs to change the way they feel. Drugs of abuse are **psychoactive substances**, meaning they change the way the brain works. If broccoli made people have out-of-body experiences or numb emotional pain, it wouldn't be so difficult to get children to eat it. (And if you're about to say that your child loves broccoli, please don't - the rest of us don't need that kind of negativity). Although people arrive at their decision to use in a variety of ways, the experience of altering their state of mind is the common thread.

Boredom & Curiosity

In some cases, kids are kids and they're bored and curious. It really can be that simple. Teens are ruled by what seems like fun. The area of their brain that is most powerful and active at this stage of life is the part of the brain that processes emotion and reward. The **prefrontal cortex** - the area that helps them to make decisions based on risk/benefit and potential outcomes - hasn't developed yet. This causes young people to make decisions based primarily on what they expect will feel good rather than what is likely to end well. Example: jumping off a roof into a pool because it makes for a great story despite the likelihood that you will break your neck if you miss.

Drug use has appeal as a standalone activity or as a way to heighten social situations. No personality or skills required! It can seem like a foolproof way to elevate enjoyable experiences or lackluster situations alike. I think you get the idea, let's move on.

Connection with peers

Captain Obvious would also point out that teens crave connection to their peers. Experimentation with alcohol or other drugs provides an opportunity to connect, especially for kids who might struggle in this department. Unfortunately, if someone was looking for an easy bake recipe for making friends, they would find it to be as simple as "just add weed". While I am saying that to be funny, it is very much a reality. I can't count how many times I've been told by teens that when they moved to a new place or were trying to make a name for themselves, they were more easily able to strike up conversations and join a peer group by talking about drug use.

This desire for connection is often framed as peer pressure. Imagining someone else's ill-intentioned child as a bad influence on ours is a convenient way to view peer pressure, but it's not really accurate. Peer pressure can certainly take the expected form of peers glorifying and encouraging use, but this is somewhat "played out," as we millennials used to say. In my years of working with teens, I have found that in large part, peer pressure comes from within.

Peer pressure is the feeling of being on the outside looking in. It can stem from hearing other teens glorifying their use and internalizing the idea that this behavior is "normal," but no one is being lured into a dark alley and forced to try something in order to be considered "cool". In large part, teens are operating on a perceived set of acceptable behaviors that they anticipate will gain them social benefit. This perception leaves them feeling that substance use is the norm and that using will align them with this apparently common behavior.

Teens expect to gain social benefit from using not only based on what their peers do and say but from our culture's glorification of substance use in mainstream media as well. The way our kids perceive things and act on their perceptions isn't the responsibility of the people around them. No matter what other people say and do around us, we have power of personal choice and can make our own decisions - no one forces us into this.

Cope with stress or uncomfortable feelings

The most common reason teens give for using is to cope with stress or discomfort. Someone somewhere wrote in the teenager bible that using will alleviate all of the common ailments of teenage life. Stressed? Take a few hits from this vape. Anxious about social situations? Numb your feelings with alcohol. Can't sleep? Marijuana will do the trick.

When I ask teens about what gave them the idea to begin using as a strategy for coping with their emotions, they often relay the conventional wisdom bestowed upon them by peers about drug use. The promise of an easier, stress-free life is made by well-meaning friends and predatory dealers alike. Unfortunately, this is the hardest myth to bust because it happens to be reinforced by the brain. The high produced by the drug numbs emotional pain, reduces inhibition, heightens positive experiences and triggers an intense reward response.

The emotional relief teens experience and the resulting reward received by the brain is incredibly powerful and difficult to argue against because the desired effect is achieved. What most young people don't realize is that using to cover up emotional discomfort does not deliver lasting relief. Instead, it backfires and leads them down a path where misery or numbing are the only options. We will talk about this in depth in Chapter 9.

Teens have a variety of reasons for experimenting with substance use. They may use to have fun, to connect with others or to problem-solve. Although it may be common for teens to try nicotine, alcohol or marijuana at some point before age 18, it is not common for their use to become regular and to interfere with their ability to function in daily life. We don't have a crystal ball to tell us whether or not this issue will escalate out of control for a particular person, so it is important to take all substance use seriously and consider how at-risk our child may be for problematic substance use. In the next section we will review what those risk factors are.

PART I:
RISKY BUSINESS

BEFORE HE PASSED, MY GRANDFATHER LOVED TO ASK ME about my work. He was curious about how people fell victim to drug use and had some of the same questions and assumptions I hear from others when they find out that I work with teens who struggle with drug use: Did their parents use drugs? Were they abused? Are they troublemakers?

As I mentioned earlier, every type of person has come through my doors, and I have met some incredible kids along the way. I have met young athletes on the verge of a professional career, straight-A students and talented musicians. I've also met determined mischief-makers, gang members with serious criminal records and everything in between. Some people I meet fit the stereotype of a drug user, but many decidedly do not.

Some of the brightest, most empathetic, talented, beautiful souls I have ever met were struggling with drug use. And that is not unique to my experience. People specializing in substance abuse treatment love doing this work because we know that anyone can get caught in this and everyone deserves help getting out.

There isn't a singular culprit to blame for a person's problematic substance use. No one circumstance, character trait or behavior can tell us who will or will not fall into this trap. When considering the likelihood that a person will begin using or the likelihood that their drug use will escalate out of control, we look at how a combination of risk and protective factors influence this process, not predict it.

Risk factors are those individual or environmental factors that increase the likelihood that someone will develop problematic substance use. In the following chapters we will explore the various risk factors teens face. As you read this section, remember that each person's level of risk is individual and results from the unique ways these factors appear in their lives.

chapter seven

AGE

THE MOST POWERFUL RISK FACTOR FOR ADDICTION IS a person's age at the time they begin using. Prior to age 25 or 26, the brain is in a state of constant growth and development, making new connections and strengthening existing ones. The brain's ability to make these changes is called **neuroplasticity**. We all have a certain degree of neuroplasticity, allowing us to integrate new information and refine skills. The developing brain, however, has a much higher degree of plasticity than that of an adult, allowing it to do these things faster and more effectively. Neuroplasticity reduces as we age, so the younger a person is, the greater degree of neuroplasticity their brain has and therefore the more quickly their brain will change.

This explains why despite snowboarding on and off for almost 20 years, I mostly tumble my way down the ski slope while my then-10-year-old son conquered intense terrain after 45 minutes in ski school. His brain was able to adapt and make new connections much faster than mine to help him learn this new skill.

This adaptability is incredibly beneficial for young people in terms of developing new skills, acquiring language and understanding the world around them. It makes their brains flexible, resilient and creative. While in those cases, neuroplasticity is a valuable contributor to their development, it is a double-edged sword. When young people experience things like traumatic stress, lack of sleep, drug use or other unhealthy influences, they can quickly develop unhealthy patterns and significant symptoms.

Healthy or unhealthy patterns and connections in the brain can be thought of as pathways. Initially, these pathways lack distinction and are not easily traveled. Like a dirt path, the connections between behaviors are initially weak. Over time, this dirt path becomes more clearly defined and direct. If behaviors are reinforced consistently enough, these pathways become like a superhighway, easily directing a person to a particular behavior. This is the case with addiction.

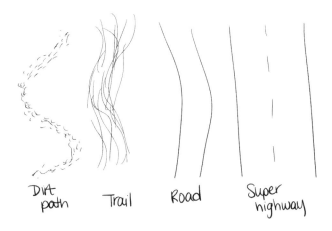

Dirt path   Trail   Road   Super highway

Addiction is a learning process that takes place as the brain develops connections specific to substance use that are reinforced with each high. Because of the developing brain's high level of neuroplasticity, it is able to create and strengthen these connections/pathways much more quickly than an adult brain, making the process of addiction play out exponentially faster for young people. This is the primary reason that risk for developing problematic use is higher for teens than for adults, but it isn't the only one.

As we just covered, the adolescent brain is in a constant state of growth and development, a process that is not complete until someone reaches age 25 or 26. The still-developing adolescent brain hasn't yet reached its potential for functioning and therefore can't do the same things an adult brain can do, plain and simple.

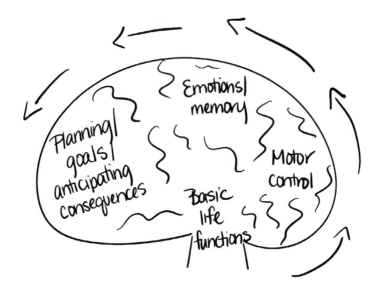

The brain develops from the bottom to top and back to front. We can think of it as developing from more basic abilities like keeping the heart beating and controlling movement to more complex abilities like managing emotions and planning. The last of our brain's capabilities to develop are our highest-order skills which include the ability to see beyond the current situation by anticipating outcomes and organizing behavior toward a goal.

The area of the brain that is last to develop is called the **Prefrontal Cortex**. The Prefrontal Cortex is the rational decision-making part of the brain. We use it to remain focused, delay gratification, anticipate outcomes and align our behavior with our goals. Without a fully functioning Prefrontal Cortex, teens chase what feels good, fail to take risks seriously and make impulsive decisions- all of which put them at risk for drug use.

I like to refer to the teen brain as the "party brain" - always looking for a good time with minimal thought about what could go wrong. So even though our kids might be the size of fully grown adults by the time they're 16, we will still be in charge of the car keys.

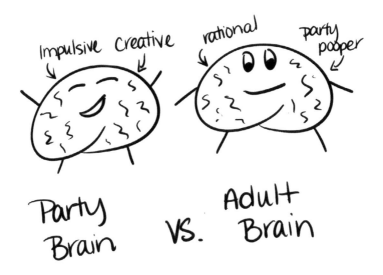

Understanding the differences between the adolescent and adult brain can help our kids make sense of a world full of contradictions. Movies and documentaries portray the harsh realities of addiction, yet advertisements glorify beer and liquor as essential party-starters. Social media makes vaping devices seem like a required accessory while researchers detail the epidemic of teen nicotine use and the severe lung injuries and illnesses that result from vaping. We are all in a confusing and difficult position, hearing opposing views on whether substance use is no big deal or a serious danger.

Marijuana is currently one of the most popular drugs of abuse among young people and is being decriminalized and legalized widely. Decriminalization and legalization have clear benefits due to the harmful, disproportionate impact criminal penalties for substance use have on low-income and minority communities. Unfortunately, there are some who promote legalization without offering a balanced perspective on the genuine risks associated with use.

Lobbyists and retailers often tout the supposed benefits of marijuana and conveniently fail to mention the serious risks that most dramatically affect teens. The heavy marketing that follows legalization and retail sales sends the overwhelming message to our kids that marijuana is generally safe.

Like any other psychoactive drug, marijuana has side effects. It suppresses activity in the parts of the brain that control learning, memory, motivation and emotional regulation.[4] In some cases, marijuana has been shown to cause **psychotic symptoms** (delusions/hallucinations) and increases risk of violent behavior.[7] Anyone who uses marijuana regularly enough for a long enough period of time will experience side effects. What is considered "enough" depends on a person's brain, body and individual risk factors.

Since these changes will happen over a much longer period of time for adults, the risks and side effects for adults are minor, especially for adults who use marijuana occasionally. Because of teens' highly adaptable, still-developing brain, the brain change and associated symptoms caused by marijuana or any other psychoactive drug occur in more dramatic fashion and over a shorter period of time than for adults. I have worked with many students who start using regularly during summer break and by winter break their attendance, grades, behavior and their mental health are noticeably suffering.

By focusing on the differences between teen and adult brains, we can better equip teens to make sense of the mixed messaging they will continue to hear about marijuana and other drugs of abuse and make a decision that is reflective of their own health rather than societal or political attitudes. Focusing on brain health also takes personal bias and judgment out of the equation. It makes the decisions we guide our children toward less about us and more about them. This is a brain health issue, plain and simple.

Quick recap - young, developing brains:

- *Are highly adaptable to new information and skills - this is called neuroplasticity.*
- *Are still in the process of developing the ability to delay gratification, manage their emotions and account for consequences in their decision-making.*
- *Develop addiction and other side effects much faster than adults.*

chapter eight

GENETICS

ANOTHER SIGNIFICANT CONTRIBUTOR TO A PERSON'S likelihood of developing an addiction is their genetics. Genetics account for up to 50% of a person's risk of developing an addiction.[5] There are a series of genetic markers that affect the way a person's brain responds to a drug and reinforces drug use behaviors. If someone has inherited a genetic predisposition for addiction, their brain will fast-track the addiction process once they begin using.

I vaguely remember lessons in science class explaining that whatever combination of a dominant (big B) trait or a recessive (little b) trait you inherited would determine traits like your hair or eye color. It's a nice, straightforward way to think about our genetics and the way we inherit traits from parents, but it is really just the beginning in terms of how genetics impact development of addiction or mental illness.

Although we can inherit a predisposition toward addiction, research into **epigenetics** (the interaction between our genetics and the environment) has shown that genetics are not puppet masters, deciding exactly how we will look, feel and behave. The National Institute on Drug Abuse explains, "that old saying 'nature or nurture' might be better phrased 'nature and nurture' because research shows that a person's health is the result of dynamic interactions between genes and the environment."[6] Our genetics affect the way our brain responds to environmental influences and our environment affects the ways our genetics are expressed.

Let's use **Schizophrenia** as an example. Schizophrenia is a mental illness that causes someone to disconnect from reality through delusions and/or hallucinations. Having a genetic predisposition for Schizophrenia increases the likelihood a person will develop this disease. Epigenetic research has helped us to understand that a genetic family history of Schizophrenia is not the only contributor to our likelihood of developing this illness. Outside influences like stress and substance use also contribute to whether or not a person develops this disorder. Marijuana use in particular increases the likelihood of developing Schizophrenia by as much as five times.[7]

Substance use is just one of many outside influences that can alter the expression of our genetics. Living in unsafe conditions, bullying, abuse, high stress and trauma, among other factors can all affect the way our genetics are expressed.[8] For better or worse our life experiences and life choices can determine what traits and tendencies will emerge.

If we experience trauma, develop a mental illness or an addiction, our genetic material reflects these changes. This means that a person who develops an addiction can then pass on a predisposition for addiction to future children. Most teens aren't thinking in terms of their legacy but it's only fair for them to have the full picture of how their behaviors impact their health and their future family's health long-term.

If you have addiction in your family history, make sure your teens are aware so they know how their genetics might affect their personal risk of developing addiction if they start using. Addiction is addiction when it comes to genetic markers, regardless of how socially acceptable that substance may be. So, if you have a family history of nicotine or alcohol addiction, that is equally as relevant as addiction to any other drug. This is all about our brain health, not about society's relationship to a particular drug. Armed with the above information, our teens can appreciate the dynamic interaction among their genetics, their environment and their behavior.

chapter nine

MENTAL ILLNESS AND TRAUMA

MENTAL ILLNESSES LIKE MAJOR DEPRESSIVE Disorder or Bipolar Disorder are diagnosed when someone experiences symptoms that impact their well-being and functioning over an extended period of time. Mental illnesses, like medical illnesses, are diagnosed based on specific signs and symptoms and can have a variety of causes. A diagnosis of a mental illness is a point-in-time description of a person's symptoms and is not static. Symptoms of mental illness and trauma may be more or less severe at certain times and may even enter remission.

The presence of mental illness or trauma is important to understanding our child's risk of problematic substance use because people struggling with these issues are at higher risk of developing substance use disorders. About half of all people experiencing a substance use disorder also experience a co-occurring mental illness (which includes trauma).[9] Co-occurring refers to the presence of more than one disease or illness.

Trauma, or Post-Traumatic Stress Disorder, is a mental illness that deserves special attention because it is has the highest rate of comorbidity with substance use disorders. Nearly half of all adults diagnosed with PTSD have a co-occurring substance use disorder. This correlation is particularly strong for adolescents with studies showing that up to 59% of young people with PTSD subsequently develop substance abuse problems.[10]

Why are these so closely related? We know that some people with trauma history use alcohol or other drugs as a way of coping with symptoms. We also know that substance use contributes to high-risk behaviors which can put people at higher risk of experiencing a traumatic event. There is also evidence that genetics are involved in this process. Childhood trauma can alter the expression of genetics and increase propensity toward substance use.[11]

The close relationship between trauma and substance use continues to be extensively researched and I encourage you to seek out more information if this applies to your child. In any case, awareness of the relationship between these two health issues adds important context to a child's individual level of risk.

Mental illness and trauma affect the way people think, feel and behave. As you can guess, people struggling to cope with their day to day due to challenging thoughts, feelings and behaviors may be understandably tempted to use alcohol or other drugs to improve their mood, quiet distressing thoughts or to alter their behavior.

Young people consistently report that their primary reason for using is to cope with stress or symptoms of mental illness. Although the idea to use drugs as a method of coping typically comes from their very wise peers, it is reinforced by a culture that values life hacks, quick fixes and magic pills.

What a tempting proposition that relief could be just moments away. We can't fault young people for wanting so badly to believe in this solution. If our kids have only been armed with judgments, opinions and fears about substance use, they don't have any ammunition to dispute the advice of others who purport to know (from experience) much better than adults who want to ruin everyone's fun.

For most people, using a drug will provide the relief from stress or discomfort they're looking for, but only in the short term. Their brain will receive a rush of dopamine, they'll feel good and disconnect from emotional pain and they will have gotten what they wanted. This leads them to believe they have successfully "self-medicated."

My dad annoyingly told me many times growing up that "if it sounds too good to be true, it probably isn't." I was so frustrated by his cynicism and lack of trust in the world. And yet, time and again the world proved him to be right. Literally every time. I think you see where I'm going with this - the idea that we can get high and forget all of our problems never to be seen or heard from again is unfortunately just way too good to be true.

If I had a dollar for every time a well-meaning parent, school counselor or even therapist told me that a child was "self-medicating" rather than suffering from a legitimate substance use problem, I would be on a beach in Hawaii instead of writing this book. Ok, I might still be writing this book, but I would be writing it on a beach in Hawaii. Since I have to listen to this nonsense without compensation, I have a strong urge to throw my shoe at anyone selling this story.

When we use the phrase "self-medicating" we send a dangerous message, implying that there is some legitimacy to the idea that using drugs will solve a child's mental health challenges. I don't blame anyone for hoping that there could be such a simple solution to what may feel like overwhelming and hopeless emotional challenges, but it's time to pull our heads out of our … sand.

We can argue about the legitimacy of certain substances like marijuana to help alleviate pain and nausea or microdosing with LSD to manage depression for adults for whom other treatments haven't worked, but our understanding of teen brain development tells us that this is not a viable solution for teens.

The skills that help us bounce back from challenges and cope with discomfort are being refined during adolescence. And the only path to developing these skills is through consistently practicing healthy strategies for coping with our emotional experience. If teens are constantly numbing or manufacturing their feelings through chemicals, their brain is not able to practice skills or build connections for healthy coping.

Mood-altering substances bypass the brain's ability to regulate and prevent healthy brain development and recovery. When substance use is a teen's primary coping strategy, they aren't able to develop the healthy pathways that allow them to cope with challenges that cause uncomfortable thoughts and feelings. The drug establishes itself as the only suitable coping strategy because the reward response from drug use is so much more powerful than other coping skills. This leads the person to believe that the only way they can manage their symptoms is by using, even when their symptoms escalate as a result of their use.

As the process of numbing with drug use and fixation on the intense reward provided by the drug plays out over time, here is what happens:

- *Motivation declines*
- *Addiction develops rapidly*
- *Social-emotional development is stunted*
- *Pre-existing symptoms of mental illness are intensified*
- *Substance-induced mental illnesses develop*

Intense emotions and ups and downs in our overall well-being are to be expected and are part of healthy human life. Especially for teenagers, emotional reactions can indicate a lack of coping skills or a response to stressors in the environment, not necessarily an illness. People often throw around words like "bipolar" or "trauma" when referring to someone's mood or behavior, but keep in mind that these are medical diagnoses. Before placing any labels on yourself or a child, seek an evaluation with a trained mental health professional. This will help you problem-solve with the most accurate picture of your health or your child's health.

A NOTE ABOUT SUICIDAL THOUGHTS:

Substance use increases the risk of suicidal thoughts and behavior for teens. Substance use intensifies emotions, interrupts the brain's ability to regulate and can increase potential for an impulsive suicide attempt. Examining the presence of any substance use is even more important if you become aware of any suicidal thoughts or feelings to gain a picture of your child's level of risk.

If your child is struggling with mental health symptoms, seeking competent care and supporting your child in building skills are substance use prevention strategies. Supporting our children with problem-solving in healthy ways can help them avoid problem-solving with substance use. To do justice to the details of how mental health and substance use interact, we will touch on this concept again later on.

Given the connection between substance use and mental illness, especially trauma, addressing them simultaneously is essential for providing competent care for people with these co-occurring conditions. Providing trauma-informed care in substance use treatment is therefore the norm. If you encounter a provider who claims that addressing trauma history or mental illness by itself will magically stop someone from using, run away - they clearly don't understand these dynamics well.

chapter ten

ACCESS

TEENS FACE RISK RELATED TO THE PEOPLE THEY ARE
in community with and are at higher risk of substance use if they spend
time with using peers. We talked already about how peer connections may
influence teen substance use but when we expand our view to include the
remainder of their immediate surroundings and community, we can see there
are a variety of people and places that enable access and opportunity for use.

If substance use is prevalent in the home, neighborhood or larger community, young people perceive substance use as less risky or even expected.
Perception of risk has a significant impact on teen use. When perception
of risk for a particular drug is high, teens are less likely to use that drug.
Conversely, when perception of risk for a particular drug is low, teens are
more likely to use it.

Just as peers can model, glorify and/or supply alcohol or other drugs,
so can older siblings, cousins, other family members and even parents. The
middle schoolers who are referred to me most often are obtaining drugs from
an older family member. Siblings and parents can contribute to risk as much
or more than other members of the community.

Project NeuroTeen, a 5-year study of adolescent relationships with
parents and peers found that "teens shift their behavior to align with the risky

choices of parents more than the risky choices of peers."[12] These findings high-light the power of parents' behavior on the decision-making and behavior of their children. They also remind us that although peer influences increase in value during the teen years, they do not necessarily hold more weight than influences from parents.

As I am writing this, we are just past Homecoming season and whenever this event and others like it roll around, I hear about parent-sponsored parties where drinking is allowed. Parents allowing their children to have alcohol in their presence, thinking that this makes their children safer, is nothing new. You may be thinking "My parents did that for me" or "I went to those parties" and you've become an incredibly successful (insert really cool job here). I get it, I went to those parties, too, and I also think I have turned out pretty well. What I would like us to consider is that these opportunities to drink under the supervision of adults did not actually reduce our overall risk of problematic use or teach us responsibility and instead gave us increased access.

Kids may be safer in a limited sense with adult supervision - they may be more likely to receive medical care for overdose or less likely to drive under the influence if they remain in the home. But the bigger picture to consider is that at an age when a child's brain is heavily impacted by addictive substances, they are provided with access and opportunity. Although we might feel that we're providing them a safe place and reducing immediate risk, we are likely adding to the list of opportunities they already have to engage in alcohol or other drug use.

Abstinence from alcohol until age 21 is an arbitrary, American idea and has changed for political reasons over time. In many cultures and countries, legal drinking ages are lower and young people can have an alcoholic beverage at dinner with their family or on special occasions. Popular belief is that these cultural attitudes toward alcohol are protective against problematic use.

My mother is from England, and I have many friends who are them-selves from other countries or whose extended family have immigrated to the U.S. For a long time I have wondered how to reconcile the very real differences in cultural attitudes toward alcohol use with the research that consistently shows age of first use as the most significant risk factor for problematic substance use. Does this research hold up around the world or does early exposure in other cultures in fact protect people? Lucky for me, I wasn't the only one with this question.

A study conducted from 1990-2016 investigated alcohol-related health outcomes across 195 countries classified as "wet" or "dry" according to their permissive or restrictive approach to alcohol use. Their findings revealed that regardless of cultural relationship with alcohol use, higher rates of alcohol use led to increased injury, disease and death. According to the authors, "Our results show that the safest level of drinking is none."[13]

The above study concludes that cultural attitudes and behaviors related to alcohol do not actually have a protective effect. More use leads to more problems, period. In fact, the only societal-level factor that did protect against negative health outcomes from alcohol use was quality of life as indicated by median income and access to healthcare.[14]

Since permissiveness and restrictiveness by themselves are not effective protection against problematic use, we can instead focus on reducing the frequency of teen substance use, which is associated with better outcomes. This means that allowing drinking at a party held in your house may be avoiding car accidents today but is not avoiding the larger problem of unhealthy drinking behavior overall. Using alcohol or other drugs negatively affects their brain whether you're there or not.[15]

Access and opportunity in the home, neighborhood and/or community places our kids at risk, so it is crucial to consider the broader context of our child's exposure. Consider the questions below and how these factors might contribute to your child's ease of access and perception of use:

- *What behaviors are older siblings engaging in? If a younger sibling is using and an older sibling is struggling, this could be an opportunity to learn more about what's going on with your older child. If you already have knowledge that an older sibling is using, are you holding them accountable or addressing it in any way that is visible to your younger child?*

- *What is your relationship like with substance use? Even if they don't see you using, are you under the influence when you're around your child? Our kids notice a lot more than we think, so even if you think it is unnoticeable, ask yourself if you want your child having the same relationship to substance use as yours.*

- *What do family gatherings or parties look like? Is there a lot of substance use going on at these events? What message might your child be receiving about how to celebrate? How much access to alcohol or other drugs do children have during these events? Is alcohol unmonitored and easily stolen?*

- *Is substance use highly visible in your community? While you can't control this, it warrants a conversation with your child about what they will encounter and how to approach situations where drugs are present or offered.*

- *How are medications stored in the home? Do teens have easy access to prescription or over-the-counter medicines? Medicines can easily become drugs of abuse when used improperly so easy access to over-the-counter or prescribed medications = risk for abuse.*

chapter eleven

THE PRIDE IS RIGHT

WHILE WE ARE ON THE TOPIC OF RISK, I WANT TO highlight that LGBTQ teens are at higher risk for developing a substance use disorder. Identifying as lesbian, gay, bisexual, transgender or questioning is not inherently a risk factor but is associated with higher rates of substance use. These teens are placed at higher risk due to the stress and trauma they experience as they navigate the world.[16]

I use the acronym "LGBTQ" at times in this chapter because this is the acronym used in the supporting literature. "LGBTQ+" is a more inclusive and accurate acronym to use but research has not accounted for all members of this community. We might assume, however, that the findings discussed in this chapter apply to other sexual minority youth as well. Research moving forward will hopefully give us a better sense of the scope of this issue for all young members of the LGBTQ+ community.

We discussed that one of the most common reasons people begin using is to cope with uncomfortable feelings. Like their peers, LGBTQ youth are at risk of problem-solving with substance use as they struggle to cope with the stressors of unsupportive and/or harmful environments. LGBTQ youth who have experienced efforts to change their sexual orientation and/or gender identity and those who had experienced physical harm due to their identity report more regular substance use.[17]

Substance use only compounds an already heightened level of mental health risk faced by LGBTQ youth. LGBTQ youth are four times more likely to attempt suicide than their **cisgender**, heterosexual counterparts. The 2021 National Survey on LGBTQ Youth Mental Health found that "Regular alcohol, marijuana, or prescription drug misuse were associated with greater odds of reporting a suicide attempt, particularly among LGBTQ youth under the age of 21".[18]

We cannot control the world our children go into or whether they are victims of discrimination, bullying or violence. But as the most powerful relationship in a child's life, we can decide that our children will not experience these stressors within the home. As our children present themselves authentically to the world, we have an opportunity to meet their vulnerability with compassion, empathy and unconditional love.

I am not an expert on LGBTQ+ teens and you don't have to be either. Children don't need us to be experts or to even fully understand their experience. They need a safe space where they can be valued simply because they exist and be free from shame. Without any specialized knowledge, we can have an impact simply by giving them space and support to learn more about who they are.

Empathic connection is a valuable tool for parents in all situations and this is no different. We may not understand our child's sense of identity or agree with it but an empathetic approach will help us work through this with them one healthy step at a time. We can value and connect with our children regardless of our own feelings and perspectives.

If you want to learn more about this topic, you can do so in a variety of ways starting with simply asking genuine, respectful questions. Seeking other personal or professional perspectives may also offer a window into this topic that your child may not be able to provide since they themselves are still figuring this out. If you are interested in learning more, I have included a list of trustworthy organizations to help you get started. These organizations provide the most current research on LGBTQ+ issues and will allow you to dive further into specific topics and connect with local resources:

- The Trevor Project is the world's largest suicide prevention and crisis intervention organization for LGBTQ (lesbian, gay, bisexual, transgender, queer, and questioning) young people. In addition to crisis support, they provide research, education and advocacy for LGBTQ youth and their families. www.thetrevor-project.org

- The American Psychological Association's webpage on Sexual Orientation and Gender Identity includes answers to common questions on the topic and a variety of educational resources - https://www.apa.org/topics/lgbtq/sexual-orientation

- Nemours' Kids Health webpage has basic information to help parents just starting their journey toward understanding sexual orientation and gender identity. https://www.kidshealth.org/en/parents/sexual-orientation.html

- The Family Acceptance Project has resources for connecting with competent care in your area. https://lgbtqfamilyacceptance.org/

- The American Academy of Pediatrics' Healthy Children site contains a variety of information and tips for parents related to sexuality and gender identity. https://HealthyChildren.org

- PFLAG provides confidential peer support, education, and advocacy to LGBTQ people, their parents and families, and allies. https://pflag.org/

chapter twelve

GATEWAY DRUG?

I CAN'T WRITE A BOOK ABOUT TEEN DRUG USE WITH-
out lending my perspective on the longstanding Gateway Drug debate. For as
long as I can remember, I've heard people debating about this topic. For my
generation, the idea of a gateway drug was specifically focused on marijuana
but for teens today I have often heard this phrase used to refer to the vaping
epidemic and nicotine addiction. My research-oriented brain has always
wondered how we could put this debate to rest - in what way can we confirm
or dispute this idea of gateway drug use? After all these years, I think I have
found a way to make sense of this for myself and for the teens I work with.
Here we go...

For background, the **Gateway Hypothesis** was introduced in 1975
by Dr. Denise Kandel in a study titled "Stages in Adolescent Involvement in
Drug Use" published in the journal Science. This groundbreaking study and
Dr. Kandel's subsequent work proposed that adolescent substance use follows
a pattern of progressive drug use starting with alcohol and nicotine, moving
to cannabis use and ultimately to use of illicit drugs like cocaine and heroin.[19]

The most common criticism of Dr. Kandel's original theory is that it
made what some believe to be too far of a leap from identifying patterns in
drug use behavior to claiming that alcohol and tobacco and marijuana themselves caused this pattern to occur. Since that time, numerous studies have

confirmed that the pattern of progressive drug use described by Dr. Kandel still holds true, but there is no conclusive evidence that specific drugs of abuse cause use of other drugs.

Research that claims to support Dr. Kandel's Gateway Hypothesis points to the neurological changes that occur as a result of regular drug use. A 2019 study which reviewed research published between 1986 and 2018 found "evidence that adolescent nicotine exposure influences long-term molecular, biochemical, and functional changes in the brain that encourage subsequent drug abuse."[20] This study shows that there may be some merit to a biological gateway due to the brain changes caused by early use.

My very basic summary of the research I've found on this topic is that researchers agree that it isn't as simple as someone using nicotine, alcohol or marijuana and then immediately being on a direct path toward use of more serious chemicals. Many teens do not escalate to use of other drugs, so it isn't a foregone conclusion that this escalation will occur.

We can't study this directly because we can't just go around giving a bunch of teenagers nicotine, alcohol or marijuana, keeping all other variables equal and then follow them to see what happens. That wouldn't exactly be ethical, now would it? Because we can only make connections and can't prove that one thing causes another, I'm not sure we'll ever be able to say with 100% certainty that any one drug is a direct gateway into other things, but even if we could I don't think it's that simple.

We very literally just finished talking about the variety of risk factors that contribute to teen drug use. Was that all just a waste of time? Of course not! Dr. Kandel's 2002 update to her hypothesis included consideration of a variety of individual and environmental influences, not just the drugs of abuse themselves. Risk factors are the variables missing from the original Gateway Hypothesis that add complexity and context to the picture of adolescent drug use.

Genetics and age can contribute on a biological level to the way in which young people respond to the intense reward provided by drug use. Mental illness and trauma can psychologically contribute to the perceived benefits or reward associated with drug use. Access in peer groups, family setting or community can make substance use an easier, more appealing option. Each of these risk factors compounds on one another. The more of these risk factors that are present, the more likely someone is to begin using and/or to quickly develop a serious problem with substance use once they begin. Additionally, the changes that occur rapidly in the brain as a result of early drug use only serve to increase sensitivity and vulnerability to drug use in general.

The most compelling research I have done on this topic has been my almost 20 years of talking to teens about their progression of drug use and what they believe is common for their peers. To help them visualize this progression, I used - you guessed it - drawings. I asked them individually or in groups to plot on a timeline the age at which different drugs entered the picture. Here is an example of the timeline I used with them showing where the responses almost always fell.

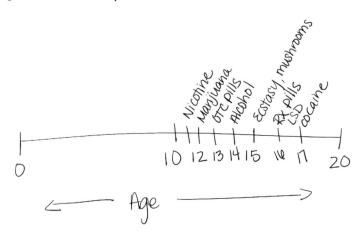

This is of course not identical for every person, but it has been amazing just how predictable this exercise became. So how did this happen? Why is this such a common progression? The message I've gotten from teens has been clear - they started using drugs that seemed low-risk, were socially acceptable and/or easy to access (almost always nicotine, marijuana and alcohol). After increasing their tolerance to a drug, they looked for a more intense high and sought out something stronger or were introduced to more serious drugs of abuse in their social network. In every discussion I've had with teens in recovery, they were adamant that early use of nicotine and marijuana led them down a path of escalating attempts to get high.

Never did I imagine that teenagers would be arguing in favor of the Gateway Hypothesis. Nor did I imagine how vehement their attitudes on the subject would be. So many teens in recovery shared just how much they wished they hadn't started using in the first place, feeling that if they hadn't had these early experiences of getting high, things could have been different for them. They feared for younger family members and younger teens in general.

After years of hearing these stories, my impression has been that the gateway might actually be the high and subsequent reward provided by drug use. Whenever I would ask teens to talk about the benefit of using, the immediate response would be "getting high". They probably thought I was stupid for even asking the question. What else would be the point anyway? So, if getting high is the whole point, then couldn't it be the act of getting high that opens doors to escalating drug use?

I believe gateway drug use can be understood as the can of worms opened when a young person with a vulnerable brain seeks out a high and receives a predictable reward response. A teen's highly adaptable brain latches on to the experience and starts to change in a way that makes them more sensitive to future drug use. Any drug of abuse would therefore be a gateway drug. It just happens to be that nicotine, alcohol and marijuana are less scary, more accessible and more socially acceptable than others, so these tend to be the first experiences young people have with being high. Then, young people with particularly vulnerable brains and circumstances (risk factors) continue seeking that experience and encounter new drugs of abuse with a brain altered to be more sensitive to substance use.

These compounding risks and brain changes create a perfect storm for quickly escalating drug use in young people. Although it is not as simplistic or easy to scare someone with, I have found that this more dynamic understanding of compounding risk and reward response as a gateway to addiction is more common-sense and sounds less like adults trying to scare kids out of experimenting with drug use.

So, if it's not as simple as we originally thought the gateway drug idea to be, how do we protect our kids or help them avoid these compounding risks? Looking back at the risk factors we've discussed; we can't do as much as we might like to control our child's relative risk. These things aren't necessarily in our control or within our child's control. What we and our children do have power over are the strengths and supports that increase their likelihood of moving through the teen years safely.

We call these strengths and supports protective factors. They are individual or environmental characteristics that reduce the likelihood that someone will develop problematic substance use. More on protective factors in Part III.

We've referenced several times that certain brain changes increase sensitivity to drug use and promote escalating attempts to get high. In the following section we will take a deeper look at what these brain changes are and how they happen.

PART II:
THEIR BRAIN ON DRUGS

ALTHOUGH USING IS A CHOICE, THE WAY OUR BRAIN responds to drug use is not. No amount of willpower or parenting can control or change this. If we as parents actually had any say at all, we would use our magical powers of control to make sure none of this could happen. It's time to let go of the notion that we might be able to puppet master our children's way out of this. We can't lock them away in castle towers and we can't put them in bubbles. What we can do is understand how this process plays out so we can give our children good information and be prepared to respond to warning signs of problematic use.

Some of us are old enough to remember ads from the 80s and 90s with metaphors for "this is your brain on drugs." Maybe you saw a commercial featuring a model trashing her kitchen or someone frying an egg. These images were memorable, for sure, but not informative. I remember getting the message that drugs were somehow bad, but I wasn't armed with any details about what exactly would happen if I used drugs. I essentially came away with the sense that someone wanted me to avoid drugs and, luckily for me, I figured they knew better than I did.

This campaign was on the right track by highlighting the negative impact of drugs on the brain, but it didn't offer any ammunition against temptation or influences from others. Just an emotionally charged warning, which we know doesn't work. By diving deeper and encouraging at least a basic understanding of the facts, this could have been a more clear, straightforward message that would have helped me make informed decisions. Instead, it relied on me believing the opinions of the ad-makers were best for me and then using that to guide my decision-making.

Most kids are much less trusting than I was. In addition, they are making decisions with the part of the brain that anticipates what will be most fun and exciting rather than what aligns with adults' recommendations. When we use good information and remove emotions from the process, we can build critical thinking skills and open a healthy dialogue. By doing this, we won't have to hope that our kids will choose to agree with the decisions we want them to make, we can prepare them to make healthy decisions for themselves.

If we as parents are going to provide the facts and focus on health in our conversations with teens, we need to have at least a basic understanding of why substance use is unhealthy for teens and what will happen if they start and continue using. This is the goal of this section - to clarify what is taking place in the brain as teens are using and how they are especially vulnerable to the brain disease of addiction.

Addiction is a learning process. It is not a choice. (Louder for the people in the back!) It is the inevitable change that our brain goes through when we introduce an addictive chemical regularly and in larger amounts. Exactly how regularly and heavily? Great question - please let me know when you figure that out.

This book would be a lot shorter and my work would be a lot easier if there was a chart with the exact frequency, quantity and length of time using a particular drug that would cause addiction. I imagine people would suffer less often from this disease if it was so clear cut. I'm sure you didn't need this book to tell you that's not how it works, but I'll tell you anyway - that's not how it works.

The real story is that addiction sneaks up on people. It starts off as the highly glorified experience we are made to believe it will always be until it leads us so far away from ourselves that we become unrecognizable. Our thoughts, mood and behavior (aka our mental health) gradually change for the worse and consequences pile up. And all of this is happening in the brain so it's incredibly difficult to put our finger on it until it turns into the stereotypical picture of addiction.

The addictive process plays out in the area of our brain known as the **limbic system**. The limbic system is known as our reward pathway. It is the part of the brain that decides which behaviors are worth repeating. **Dopamine** is the **neurotransmitter** (chemical messenger) responsible for sending this reward message to our brain. When we experience pleasure, our brain produces Dopamine, which sends a chemical message to our brain that the behavior is rewarding and therefore worth repeating.[21]

Our brain releases its own, home-made Dopamine when we engage in positive experiences like spending time with friends & family, playing a sport or doing something creative, among others. This natural, healthy boost of dopamine received from enjoyable activities reinforces these behaviors, motivating us to continue them, and - very importantly - assigns a value to these activities. Behaviors that stimulate a Dopamine release are therefore those behaviors that we are motivated toward and place value on.

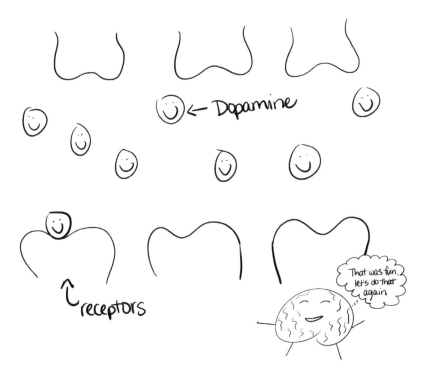

To summarize, Dopamine has 3 important functions:

- *Identifies the reward from a pleasurable experience*
- *Motivates people toward a behavior*
- *Assigns value to an activity*

Mood-altering chemicals, like nicotine, alcohol and others, provide a larger and more reliable boost of Dopamine than is naturally produced by the brain during pleasurable activities. When the brain is flooded with Dopamine after using a drug, the reward response is a guarantee, and who doesn't love a sure thing? This intense, sure-fire reward motivates the person to continue use and assigns a higher value on drug use than other behaviors that provide a less of a Dopamine release.

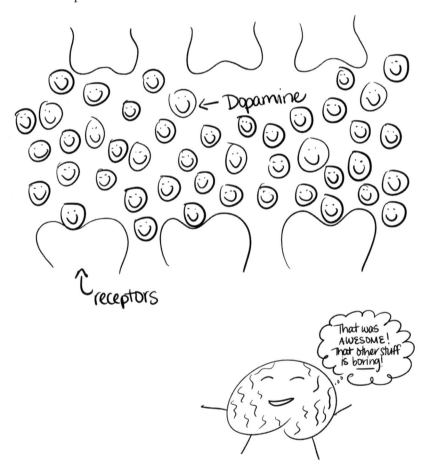

After receiving these large, artificial boosts of Dopamine over a period of time, the brain becomes overwhelmed and overstimulated. To cope with this, the brain responds by producing less and less of its own Dopamine. In addition to producing less of its own Dopamine, the structures that receive the chemical message from Dopamine are damaged. Both of these changes cause our motivation for anything other than drug use to decline as our brain does not receive the same pleasure and reward response it once did from those experiences. It also causes us to experience tolerance to the drug - needing larger amounts to feel the same effect or receiving less of an effect when using the same amount.[22]

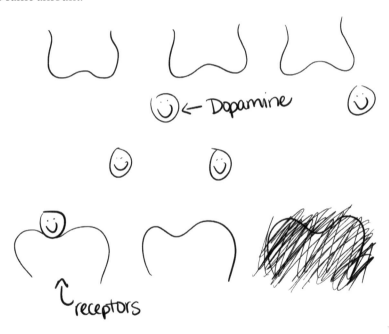

As the limbic system motivates the person toward drug use and places a higher value on drug use than other behaviors, substance use becomes increasingly compulsive. The person's decision-making is now driven more by the brain's pleasure/reward response and less by logic, goals or previously held value systems. The limbic system is focused on immediate gratification and short-term pleasure - it does not concern itself with goals or consequences that lay further down the road.

What we've already learned about adolescent brain development is now really important. As we discussed during the chapter on risk factors, the part of the brain that takes consequences and long-term outcomes into account (the prefrontal cortex) is not yet developed. An adult with a fully developed prefrontal cortex is much more capable of overriding the impulses of the limbic system than a teen who most often uses the limbic system to guide decision-making. Our knowledge of neuroplasticity also tells us that these limbic system changes are going to happen very quickly in the teen brain.

Since we aren't yet able to do regular checkup-style brain scans to assess the functioning of our teens' brains and limbic systems, how are we to know that these changes are taking place? Luckily, or unluckily, their mood and behavior will present us with clues. We will explore these warning signs and symptoms in Part V. Let's review a few key points before we move on.

Repeated use of mood-altering chemicals negatively impacts the brain's reward system in a few different ways:

- *The brain produces less of its own Dopamine as the regular, artificial boost of Dopamine provided by the person's drug use is larger and more reliable*

- *The brain's Dopamine receptors become damaged and therefore unable to receive the chemical message of pleasure/reward sent by the limited amount of Dopamine being produced*

- *Tolerance for the drug increases and larger amounts of the chemical are needed to experience the same level of pleasure*

These changes to the limbic system cause the following:

- *Reduced pleasure from previously enjoyable activities*

- *Increased motivation and value for drug use behaviors*

- *Increasingly compulsive drug-seeking behavior*

PART III:
HEALTHY KIDS

WE HAVE COVERED SOME OF THE MOST PROFOUND factors influencing risk for substance use, but we know that not everyone facing these risks develops a problem with substance use. Although we don't have control over whether our child struggles with a mental illness, what genetics they inherited or who they surround themselves with, there is a great deal we can do to help them mitigate these risks and prepare them for a life that doesn't involve drugs.

Parents make a career out of avoiding or removing obstacles for our children. From literally moving objects that could harm them when they're young to advocating for accommodations and supports that will help them succeed, we are right there to streamline their path to success and protect them from harm. Often, this looks like discouraging certain friendships, saying 'no' to sketchy plans or monitoring communications through apps downloaded onto their phones. While these are reasonable and beneficial efforts to make, avoiding risk or removing barriers entirely is not possible.

To really set our children up for success, we need to prepare our kids to deal with barriers and risky situations in a healthy way. Investing in our children's resiliency skills and connection to the world around them will get them so much farther than us acting like bouncers at Club Brain. Known as **protective factors**, these are strengths that we can foster in our children's lives so that they are able to overcome the roadblocks or risky situations that we can't keep them from encountering.

There are many theories and programs with their own take on the protective factors associated with reducing substance use. I imagine that by the time I could list them all someone would have created yet another way to conceptualize it. And it really depends on how detailed we want to be.

We could list every small facet of someone's personality or experience that contributes to their overall well-being, because healthier, happier people are less likely to engage in substance use. But as they say, "We're here for a good time, not a long time," so we will approach this with simple, broad strokes.

chapter thirteen

MEET ME AT THE INTERSECTION

MENTAL HEALTH HAS DESERVEDLY RECEIVED A GREAT deal of attention in popular culture recently. And with heavy use of any word or phrase, the meaning can become diffuse. For our purposes, a person's **mental health** refers to their emotional, psychological and social well-being.[23] It helps determine how we handle stress, relate to others, and make healthy choices. Mental health is not something we inherently do or do not have; it is something we do or do not practice.

Even though we talk about feelings as if we do, we don't have stress, anger or happiness - they are not permanent fixtures to keep. We experience feelings more or less intensely and for shorter or longer periods of time based on the way we interpret and respond to our surroundings and inner experience. Like our feelings, our mental health is not something we are born with nor is it a character trait. It is the sum of our attitudes, skills, behaviors and connections. How we use those attitudes, skills, behaviors and connections contributes to the ever-fluctuating state of our mental health.

We discussed mental illness as a risk factor that plays a role in young people developing substance use disorders. And it's easy to think of mental health as the opposite of mental illness, but this is not the case. I want us to be careful not to view mental health as just the flip side of the mental illness coin because doing so doesn't do justice to this important health concept and valuable protective factor.

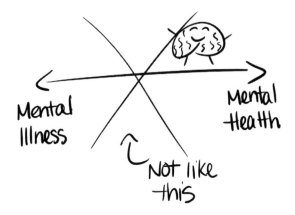

Mental health and mental illness are not opposite ends of a spectrum. They are distinct concepts that intersect to contribute to our overall mental well-being. The highly scientific drawing below shows this intersection with mental health and mental illness each on its own axis. At any given time, we experience a greater or lesser degree of overall well-being based on where we fall on each axis.

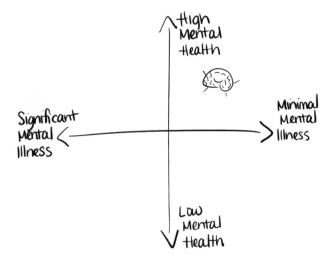

The mental illness axis includes a spectrum of experiences ranging from no symptoms of mental illness to severe, debilitating symptoms that interrupt the ability to function. Someone diagnosed with an illness like Generalized Anxiety Disorder can experience a range of symptoms. Minimal symptoms of mental illness for someone with anxiety might look like worried thoughts that are easily refuted or controlled, causing little to no impact on their functioning or enjoyment of life. At the other end of this spectrum, people suffering from severe anxiety symptoms such as panic attacks can experience significant disruption to their day-to-day life, potentially stopping them from leaving the house or engaging in social activities.

Mental illness presents differently for different people. And even for a single individual, these illnesses can present differently at different points in time. Depending on a variety of factors, the severity of someone's mental illness can change during a given day, week, month or year.

Our level of mental health also changes day-to-day and throughout our life depending on the way we respond to stressors, practice self-care, utilize coping skills and connect to supports. Because our mental health is influenced by factors within and around us, it is constantly evolving as we succeed or struggle to use our skills and resources to respond to the challenges we face.

The way we take care of our mental health by using these skills and connections helps or hinders us in managing everyday challenges and coping with symptoms of mental illness. Someone with a high degree of mental health will be able to navigate everyday challenges as well as mitigate and manage symptoms of mental illness. People who have not developed strong mental health skills or made healthy connections may be overwhelmed easily by symptoms of mental illness and common stressors alike.

We would all like to be in the high mental health, minimal mental illness quadrant of this graph. And for some of us, on our good days, this is the case. In this quadrant, we feel at our best and are able to tackle a variety of challenges and still function well.

Looking clockwise at our graph, someone experiencing minimal symptoms of mental illness but who has minimal mental health skills and supports would still likely struggle with common daily challenges. Although they may not be challenged by symptoms of mental illness, they lack the skills and support to overcome typical stressors.

In the bottom left quadrant, people with a high level of mental illness combined with minimal mental health skills/supports would be often in crisis. They would be easily overwhelmed both by everyday challenges and by specific symptoms of their illness. These are people most likely to need crisis intervention services.

Finally, someone experiencing a moderate to high level of mental illness but strong mental health skills and supports would be able to cope with their symptoms and stressors effectively. They would be able to recognize and apply coping skills to symptoms to reduce their impact on their lives. These are people we describe as in recovery. In recovery, people do not simply stop having symptoms. They have skills, strategies and supports that allow them to manage their thoughts, feelings and behaviors in a healthy way, leading to a reduction in symptoms and improved state of well-being.

To illustrate this point about intersectionality in mental health and mental illness, I'd like to share a story of my own. I have a specific fear of heights, which on most days I can easily manage. I can refute irrational thoughts in order to enjoy activities that provoke worry like standing on a ladder to put up Christmas lights or riding a roller coaster with my kids. So, generally speaking, I fall in the low mental illness, high mental health section of our graph. But that is of course not the case in this story.

Once upon a time, for a friend's birthday celebration, my husband and I went to New York City and did what New Yorkers do (or at least what these New Yorkers do). On the first night, we went to our friend's party and then ate what I am going to call "second dinner" at 3am, finally returning to our hotel room at 5am. For some reason I did not sleep at all. Like, AT ALL.

We got an early start the next day and after a long day of sight-seeing, I was an exhausted wreck. That night at dinner, the idea of visiting a lounge on the 101st floor of some god-forsaken building came up and morphed into a definitive plan to the delight of everyone but me. Mustering all of the mental health skills in my toolbox, I tried to stay calm and appear to be a completely normal, non-terrified human person. I breathed deeply, refuted irrational fears about the structural integrity of tall buildings and made a plan to stay away from windows.

After a comically stress-inducing ride in an LED-covered elevator, we made it to the 101st floor of said god-forsaken building. Stepping off the elevator, the view was absolutely incredible - for the 1.3 seconds I was able to take it in. Following my plan, I turned toward the interior wall to talk to someone and pretend I was in a completely average place much lower to the ground. And then it happened ... I felt the building move.

Is it realistic to perceive the movement of a tall building? I don't know, but my anxiety certainly thought so. The rational part of me knows that tall buildings are designed to be flexible and move, so even if my perception of movement was real, it was perfectly normal. This did not matter one bit. In that moment I felt in my soul that the building was falling and we would all plummet to an untimely death. I panicked. Full. Blown. Panic. Continuing with my plan, I asked the hostess to direct me to the bathroom so I could gather myself.

Where was that bathroom you ask? Around a narrow corner, along a 6ft-wide hallway across from floor-to-ceiling windows revealing my certain doom.

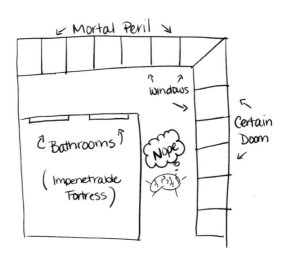

Exhausted and at my wit's end, I'd had enough. I walk-of-shame-ed myself to the hostess who kindly ushered me in to the elevator from hell which whisked me back to solid ground where I was able to regain clarity and calm.

An important lesson I learned from having children is that I do not function well without sleep. I know this experience would almost certainly have gone differently had I not been exhausted or had the bathroom been LITERALLY ANYWHERE ELSE. (I mean, honestly, why?!)

My mental health was clearly impacted that night by these factors, placing me further toward the high mental illness, low mental health section of the graph in that particular situation. As a result, I didn't cope well. Had we visited that lounge on a day when I was feeling my best, I may have been able to keep my anxiety at bay enough to stay and enjoy my time with friends. But we'll never know, will we? #notgoingback

I imagine that you have your own story of a time when individual challenges or environmental factors affected your ability to cope with a situation that you might otherwise have been able to manage well. So, how do your mental health skills and symptoms (or lack thereof) intersect? Try plotting yourself on the graph below to show how your unique level of mental health and mental illness intersect today. Then, consider how this was different at another time in your life and how that affected your ability to respond effectively to the situation you were in.

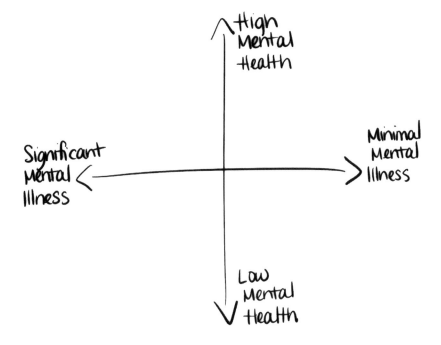

We can use this idea of intersectionality to help us understand our own well-being and that of our children. It can help us identify what we do and do not have power over. Environmental stressors or automatic negative thoughts might not be within our control so we can give ourselves some grace when we struggle more as a result. On the other hand, we do have the ability to change the decisions we make about how we respond to challenges, which amounts to our mental health. So, how do get our hands on some of this mental health we've been talking about? Funny enough, there's a chapter for that.

chapter fourteen

BUILDING MENTAL HEALTH

I OFTEN HEAR PEOPLE REFERRING TO MENTAL HEALTH skills as those coping skills that become relevant when our emotions are heightened or we are struggling with symptoms of mental illness. But mental health skills and resiliency-building are important for everyone. These skills are critical for us to be at our best every day and to prevent us from becoming overwhelmed by symptoms and/or stressors. If we are actively practicing mental health and remaining connected on a regular basis, we can prevent those crisis moments when we would otherwise hope our emergency coping skills would kick in.

In therapy, I refer to this process of taking charge of our mental health as choosing to be a thermostat instead of a thermometer. I know I am not the only person to use the concept of an emotional thermostat or thermometer, but I can't quite find a singular original source on this, so let's just leave it at 'someone much smarter than me came up with this and I really like it.'

Thermometers react to the temperature that they encounter. Being a thermometer from a mental health perspective means that your well-being is dependent upon what is happening around you. In this case, your internal experience is highly dependent on factors in your environment that are completely out of your control, meaning you do not have good control of your

64

well-being. This causes people to struggle to make progress because their success or lack thereof is determined by external variables.

Being a mental health **thermostat** means that you take charge of your well-being by practicing self-care, maintaining healthy connections and tackling stressors proactively. This is what therapy is really all about. Not everyone who comes to therapy is experiencing mental illness. People come to therapy to solve a problem and improve their well-being, which means building their mental health skills.

In therapy, the goal is not necessarily to take away the reason someone came for help. The work that happens in therapy can help the brain heal in powerful ways, but we do not aim to erase symptoms, remove stressors or undo trauma. Instead, we empower people to build resiliency and enhance their mental health. In doing so, they are able to manage the challenges they face in a healthier way, reducing the impact of mental illness and/or external stressors. This process of building mental health skills and connections translates to becoming a mental health thermostat.

Supporting your child in building mental health skills regardless of their experience of any mental illness will be incredibly protective. As adults, we often take for granted these skills that help us relate to others, understand ourselves and adapt to our environment. But like any other skill, they need to be learned. This process of building mental health and relationship skills is often referred to as **social emotional learning**.

Remember when we talked about pathways in our brain developing from dirt roads to superhighways? This is the case with mental health and relationship skills. The more they are practiced, the more internalized they are and the more automatic they will become. As our children age and practice these healthy skills, they will become increasingly adept at these skills and their abilities will become more sophisticated.

We can liken our developing brain to that of a growing tree. Think of the tree's branches as the connections and pathways to mental health skills. When a tree is in its early stages, it has few branches. Likewise, our children have few skills early on and the skills they have are somewhat primitive. As the tree grows, more branches/leaves form and the network of branches becomes more complex. This growth comes about through consistent practicing of healthy self-care, connections and coping. Building these resiliency skills does not happen by accident.

How can we help our children get to this point where they have an array of strong pathways for resilience? I am often asked by parents what professionals are doing or can do to teach children to be mentally healthy. Although the process of providing therapy requires training and is part science, part art form, mental health skills themselves are not rocket science. We have opportunities to learn and practice these skills just about every day as we work through challenges big and small. Everywhere your child spends time they have an opportunity to practice these skills.

Because young people spend so much of their time in school and because these skills are so beneficial to academic success, school systems are increasingly utilizing formal programming for social and emotional learning (SEL). The school setting creates natural opportunities to build resiliency in social contexts. Students can practice healthy interactions with peers and adults, cope with stressors and problem-solve in real time, so it makes sense we would implement these programs in the school setting. Social emotional learning is valuable in the school setting, but parents have an equally if not more important role to play in helping their children develop healthy attitudes, behaviors and relationships.[24]

Modeling, actively teaching and practicing social emotional skills with your child at home is as valuable as teaching good manners, personal hygiene and study skills. To provide a solid foundation for your child's growth, you are going to need to be well-versed in these skills yourself. Take a moment and think about where you stand with this. You might try answering these questions:

- *How do you monitor your own reactions and thoughts?*
- *What helps you gain a healthy perspective?*
- *How do you respond to stressful life events?*
- *What do you do to take care of yourself?*
- *Who are your trusted supports?*
- *How do you value yourself and set boundaries with others?*
- *How do you respond to conflict with others?*

As the saying goes, you can't pour from an empty cup, so it is incredibly relevant here whether or not you as the parent have a repertoire of mental health knowledge and skills that you can pass on to your children. If after taking a good hard look in the mirror you realize that you don't have a solid skill set to model, then there's no time like the present to take the steps to improve your skills. The act of seeking this self-improvement is itself good modeling for your children.

Below are some of the key skills I focus on with clients in therapy. These can give you some direction about what to work on for yourself and with your children:

- *Set and maintain healthy boundaries with others*
- *Connect with people in different parts of your life*
- *Choose your thoughts as carefully as you would choose your words with someone you care about*
- *Take care of your physical health*
- *Make time for hobbies/interests that you enjoy*
- *Do something that gives you a sense of accomplishment*
- *Practice gratitude daily and be specific about what you are grateful for*
- *Incorporate a few healthy routines and rituals to provide stability*
- *Identify goals and take small steps toward them*
- *Identify values and priorities and use those to guide your decisions.*

Mental health skills are neither complex nor mysterious and you will find mental health advice just about everywhere you go in real life or on the internet. I can't even venture a guess as to how many books, blog posts, social media posts, articles, seminars or other content exist in the Pop Psychology world where you can go to find tips for building mental health skills for yourself and your children. Keep in mind that it is not a replacement for therapy. It does not offer individualized support and education.

We're going to have to leave this chapter feeling somewhat unfinished because sharing the intimate details of every possible mental health concept would be another book or series of books entirely. If you feel that your mental health skills need some improvement or you are struggling with a specific issue, I suggest seeking out a trained professional. I know, I'm biased, but a professional will be able to take your unique circumstances into account and help you develop strategies and solutions tailored to your needs.

A NOTE ABOUT MENTAL HEALTH MEDICATIONS:

Mental health medications are incredibly powerful tools for reducing symptoms of mental illness and for some people are a crucial aspect of their overall wellness. If you are considering or are already taking mental health medications, I hope you will keep in mind that medications only address one component of the intersection of our mental health and mental illness. Medicines may alleviate or help manage symptoms of mental illness, but they cannot manifest mental health. They can't help us set boundaries with other people or call a friend when we need to talk. They can't make us prioritize our physical health or reframe unhelpful thoughts. And for this reason, they will always fall short of being a singular fix for us to live our healthiest, happiest life. Research consistently shows that the combination of therapy and mental health medications is more effective than medication alone.

chapter fifteen

HEALTHY CONNECTIONS

HEALTHY CONNECTIONS ARE ANOTHER IMPORTANT protective factor for children and teens and come in all forms. They include family, friends, mentors, school staff, coaches, spiritual leaders and more. They are those who guide and encourage us and who sit in the mud puddle of life with us, offering a beacon of hope in difficult times. The powerful connections we make with others are as much a contributor to our success as our own fortitude and talent.

I challenge you to think of a time you experienced personal growth or overcame an obstacle without the help of another person in one way or another. The support we receive from others is a significant contributor to our overall well-being and resiliency. We can do difficult things and succeed in the face of adversity, but we rarely, if ever, do so alone.

Can you think of a more powerful connection than that of a parent and child? Not all connections between parents/caregivers and the children they raise are healthy, but all are powerful. According to the Substance Abuse and Mental Health Services Administration (SAMHSA), effective parenting has been shown to mediate the effects of multiple risk factors for substance use and mental illness.[25]

From parents, children learn whether or not the world is a safe and trustworthy place and whether or not they are a valued part of that world. They don't inherently know how we feel about them - their understanding of our love and appreciation for them is learned. From birth, we have to nurture and earn a healthy connection through safety, love and empathy. This healthy connection forms the basis for structure, accountability and support. Connection before content!

The foundational connection between children and their parents enables children to go out into the world and find other relationships to support and uplift them as well. The Centers for Disease Control reports that "youth who feel connected at school and home are less likely to experience negative health outcomes related to sexual risk, substance use, violence, and mental health."[26] Given that young people spend such a large amount of their time in school and in school-related activities, it makes sense that connectedness in the school setting is as beneficial to their health as connections at home.

Take notice that this statement is very broad. Connectedness at school can be found in a number of ways and is unique to each person. Some children and teens form positive relationships with teachers, some with administrators, coaches or other faculty they see in the building. One student recently told me that his trusted adult in the building was one of the janitors. Healthy connections are beneficial no matter where they are found.

In addition to finding trusted adults and mentors in the school setting, young people spend time with classmates and have access to a number of clubs, student organizations or extracurricular activities. Engaging in these offerings at school, even if your child is new to the activity or idea, can help them develop relationships with their peers and strengthen their sense of belonging in the school community. Encouraging regular attendance at school and active engagement with peers and adults alike will help your child build a community of support that benefits them now and into the future.

Young people have any number of opportunities to find healthy relationships at home, in school and in their community. Not everyone will find connection in the same ways or have the healthiest connection options available to them. What is most important is that they find connection somewhere and that they learn the skills they need to establish and maintain these valuable relationships.

Wherever your child finds connection- whether it is in the context of school, hobbies, religious organizations, extended family or peer networks- your engagement remains valuable. The way you interact with people both inside and outside of your family sets an important precedent for how your child will relate to others. If you want your child to be well-connected and supported, then you, too, should be involved and practice healthy communication within these networks.

In his 2015 TED talk, best-selling author Johann Hari described that "the opposite of addiction is not sobriety, the opposite of addiction is connection."[27] If he is right, then helping our children establish and maintain positive connections might just be one of the most important things we can do to protect them from developing problems with substance use.

chapter sixteen

ACCOUNTABILITY

ONCE UPON A TIME WHEN I WAS A BABY THERAPIST, I was expressing to my supervisor my feelings of failure following a client's relapse. Her response to me has stuck with me and changed my life personally and professionally. She challenged me by asking, "Would you be taking credit if they were successful?" I replied, "of course not, they had to do the work." She explained that if I take responsibility for my client's difficulties, making it about me, I will similarly have to take credit for their successes.

This was a pivotal moment in my career, and I am forever grateful to her for shifting my thinking in this way. Understanding that taking ownership of someone else's struggles meant likewise taking credit for their triumph has helped put me in my place so I can help others while respecting their ability to help themselves.

Accepting responsibility for our actions can be uncomfortable but it is empowering. If a person is responsible for their choices, they are in charge of their change. Holding children accountable to their actions promotes a growth mindset in which they have the ability to make change and chart a new course. Then when they succeed, they can own their accomplishments and reflect on their strengths, skills and decisions with pride.

Accountability at home is protective against multiple teen health problems, including teen substance use, according to the CDC.[28] Accountability helps our children practice anticipating outcomes and making connections between their behavior and rewards or consequences. This practice helps them develop healthy decision-making skills and strengthen the part of their brain that aids in decision-making. It also makes it easier for us to respond early to any substance-related behaviors and intervene before things get out of hand.

Please note the use of the word response rather than reaction. When our rules are clear, our responses are predictable and our actions are consistent, we don't need to rely on the intensity of our emotion to tell children where they stand with us. In fact, relying on intense emotional reactions will cause our kids to focus more on our emotions and behavior than on their own. Remaining in control of yourself as you implement responses/consequences will help keep the focus on their choices. More on this in Chapter 20, Everyone remain calm.

Responses to behavior should be well-balanced, giving as much focus to behaviors we want to reinforce as to behaviors we want them to avoid or discontinue. I have met parents who are skilled at implementing consequences but underestimate the power of consistently praising or rewarding positive behaviors. If our kids know what behaviors are expected or preferred and know what positive outcomes they will enjoy as a result, they are more likely to strive toward those healthy behaviors. Positive reinforcement of healthy choices is as critical to accountability as consequencing unhealthy ones.

If we avoid holding our children accountable, we rob them of the ability to take control of their own lives and actually stand in the way of their growth and change. Instead of empowering them, we are enabling them. **Enabling** inadvertently promotes unhealthy behaviors because the enabled person avoids painful consequences that could have helped them to learn and redirect their decision-making. While it is a natural instinct to protect someone you love from pain, especially a child, doing so handicaps their ability to connect decisions with their outcomes. This in turn causes them to have difficulty creating solutions to problems.

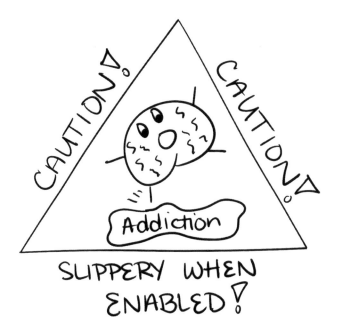

An enabled teen who is using will only encounter increasingly painful consequences, some even life-threatening but will not have the tools to resolve them, to make things right or find their way back to themselves. And ultimately, they will face consequences that parents are unable to save them from. Serious consequences that can include serious injury, jail or death. Now, that sounds really intense. And unfortunately it is.

Kids have lots of tricks up their sleeve with the goal of manipulating us into accepting their behavior. Some are easy to recognize while others are such evil genius that they can tug on our heartstrings just enough to draw us in.

Here are a few examples:

- *You try to put shoes on your toddler before leaving the house. You are now dubbed "the meanest _____ ever".*

- *You provide a completely reasonable consequence to your 4th-grader and they "don't want to be in this family anymore"*

- *You set a curfew for your 10th grader and they tell you that no one else's parents care when they get home.*

Sound familiar? Although the messages are increasingly specific, they are equally full of nonsense and all have the same purpose - to throw you off track and alter your behavior through self-doubt. If you come face to face with one of these arguments, stand your ground in the same way you would if a toddler was telling you that brushing their teeth is not necessary.

The vast majority of teens I work with have grown up in at least two cultures. While their parents try to raise them with values and expectations they hold dear, children living in households with first generation American parents are expected to blend in with a predominantly white, western value system. I have had many frustrated parents in my office saying that their child tells them, "American parents let their kids [insert ridiculous thing here]." They claim that American parents don't care to meet friends or other parents, don't keep tabs on their children, don't ask where they're going, don't set curfews and so on.

This is just one of many versions of the smokescreen that all American children tell their parents, which goes, "everyone else's parents let their kids [insert ridiculous thing here]." The intent here is not simply to inform parents about the inner workings of families more perfect than theirs, but instead to spark self-doubt and manipulate parents into allowing them to get their way.

Even if, in some universe, your child truly has befriended one or more of the very few children whose parents have no rules or consequences, this is not reason to allow the same. In fact, it might mean that your child needs boundaries and accountability even more. If your teen doesn't want to accept the boundaries you have set, here is my advice: talk less. It is not necessary or helpful to try to lecture or explain yourself until they agree with you. No one is buying a ticket to your TED talk here. The limits are the limits and the response is the response. When you have set boundaries as a parent, you can give your reasoning in a brief statement and leave it at that. No further explanation needed.

Here are some tips for increasing or maintaining accountability with your kids:

- *Set clear boundaries and expectations - It should be very clear, possibly even in writing, what the expectations are in your home. Having limits made as clear as possible in advance will allow your child to know exactly where they stand with their behavior and if they are crossing a line. It will also mean you can talk less and act more if a boundary is crossed.*

- *Match behaviors with clear, predictable responses - Make sure your child knows with certainty that if X happens, Y will follow. Being able to predict outcomes will help them develop and strengthen this skill and will allow them to incorporate this knowledge of outcomes into their refusal skills in risky situations.*

- *Scale responses appropriately - Responses to behavior (both positive and negative) should reflect the level of positive or negative impact of that behavior. Helping a sibling accomplish a task? Awesome! Creating a food drive to donate to homeless people during the holidays? Majorly awesome! Acting disrespectfully? You're in trouble. Get caught sneaking out? You're in big trouble. Exactly which behaviors hold more weight and what those responses will look like is based on your family's values and what you can realistically implement.*

- *Be consistent - Clear rules and projected outcomes are great, but none of this is helpful if you don't consistently respond in the way you intend to. Consistent responses will demonstrate that you are safe and trustworthy. Talking about these plans with other parenting partners will help protect accountability between and within households.*

- *Trust but verify - Trust is not an entitlement. It is earned through consistently honest, reliable words and actions. Trust is a dynamic process that can ebb and flow based on those words and actions.*

Think of it like an accordion. Your accordion of trust will contract or expand depending on whether your child's words and actions match. Providing smaller amounts of trust and then verifying that they have appropriately managed that level of trust allows you to build to the next level of trust.

If you feel like you're in a runaway train scenario and are trying to create increased accountability amidst anarchy in the home, keep going. No one wants accountability but we all need it. Starting this process of breaking enabling patterns and creating accountability at home is exhausting and you will be tested by young people with much more energy than you.

Don't be discouraged if things seem like they get a little worse or more intense as you are setting up a new way of doing things. Change is hard and sometimes the resistance to change can intensify things before it gets better. But if you stay the course and invest in this accountability, you will help protect your kids and make your life easier in the long run.

PART IV:
HAVING "THE TALK(S)"

ONE OF THE MOST SURPRISING THINGS THAT HAS HAPpened in my career has been that the young people I work with tell me about their "Inner Fiona". The first time I heard this was a year or two after finishing graduate school and working with teens in substance abuse treatment groups. A young man came in to meet with me and was talking about how his week had been. He was recounting an event where he was offered marijuana and wanted to accept. He said, "You ruined it for me, because I heard your voice in my head telling me this was going to end badly and I couldn't enjoy it."

First of all, I admit I was ecstatic to hear this. But once my ego relaxed a bit, I realized that this really wasn't me. He had internalized changes to his thought process during treatment and this was how he made sense of it.

Stories like this have continued over the past 15 years. Because my teenage clients most often call me "Ms. Fiona," they refer to the internalized ideas, information and soundbites from therapy as their "inner Fiona." Clients internalizing what I say or what they learn in therapy doesn't happen because I am a uniquely skilled therapist, it happens because I am a consistent and predictable one.

In various treatment settings, I have spent at most 15 hours per week with teens in treatment. So, if my predictability during a small window of time allows teens to internalize the ideas and feedback we discuss, imagine what your children are already internalizing from the many interactions you have with them as a powerful agent of change in their life.

I've had many moments when one or both of my children gave a response to something exactly like the one I always would. Sometimes I'm incredibly proud and sometimes I think "oh no I hope you don't say that at school." For better or worse, our kids are listening to and internalizing the things we say and do consistently. So, will we use this power for good or for evil?

It might not always feel like it, but a parent's opinion does matter. It matters a lot. Maybe even to the point of our children becoming angry and defensive whenever they feel judged or disrespected. If you've been in a heated exchange with your child who feels judged when you tell them their behavior is unacceptable then take a moment and pat yourself on the back because they are letting you know that your opinion is important enough to them to feel offended when you don't approve.

This is where we hold our power. In the context of our relationship with our children we can educate, motivate, correct and support them (connection before content!). With the background knowledge of how substance use affects the brain, what places young people at risk and what can protect against it, it's time to make a plan for discussing this topic with our kids.

The elements of successful dialogue we will cover are not for a one-time talk. This is an ongoing process that evolves as our children age and new information becomes more relevant. This will be a regular check-in and point of discussion. We will not be having "the talk," we will be having "the talks."

chapter seventeen

TALK EARLY AND OFTEN

WHEN I WAS A NEW MOTHER, I READ TRACY HOGG'S *Secrets of the Baby Whisperer*. In it, she encourages parents to "start as you mean to go on".[29] Her recommendation was to engage with your child in a way that you want to continue long-term even though it may be more challenging in the present. I think we should take this to heart when it comes to substance use as well. If we want our kids to talk to us about this issue in the future, we've got to start having those conversations early (in an age-appropriate way) and set a tone in these conversations that encourages ongoing dialogue. It also means we will need to set clear boundaries and expectations that will be enforced moving forward.

I don't believe it is ever too early to talk about substance use with our kids. Color me biased, but at any age there are appropriate ways to provide this health education. You wouldn't tell a 5-year-old every detail about how babies are made or what happens when someone dies, so you likewise aren't going to discuss the entire depths of addiction and drug abuse with them. You can start with basic, age-appropriate information and add detail and context to your conversations over time.

Take some time to think about what attitude you want to portray to your child about this issue. What do you want them to anticipate your response will be if they tell you they're considering using or have already done so?

Consistently approaching early conversations with honesty and empathy will make later interactions feel more comfortable and natural.

Early conversations about substance use should not only be fact-based and health-focused, they should also make clear the expectations in your household. We talked about accountability as a protective factor and how the predictability of being held accountable in your home will help your child make healthier choices. How you forecast your response to any warning signs of substance use early on will prepare you and your child for what is to come if warning signs emerge. Following the guidelines shared in the chapter on accountability will help you formulate a solid plan.

Getting ahead of this issue early is a great idea, but this isn't always the case. Frankly, this book exists because of the reality that many people just don't see the need to start these conversations early and others don't foresee having these conversations at all.

Maybe your first child worked through this issue with ease, and you didn't need such a clear plan for these interactions. Maybe you are discovering this idea about proactive engagement and playing catch-up. Sometimes parenting plans change based on new information or the needs of different children. In these cases, I encourage you to take a look at what needs to be done now and give yourself permission to change direction mid-stream. Just because things have been done a certain way until now doesn't mean you can't chart a new course that better serves you and your family.

Taking a breath to step back and plan out a new way of doing things is a valuable investment of your time and energy. It might pose challenges at first but will yield long-term benefit if you are able to refocus your efforts to be more proactive.

chapter eighteen

EMPATHY

MY CAREER HAS BEEN SPENT ALMOST ENTIRELY WITH teens and the more time I spend with them, the more amazed I am by their awareness and connectedness to the world around them. Not to mention they are tackling an increasingly complex environment with more compassion and drive to change it than any of my peers did at their age. I can't say that high schoolers of my generation were raising awareness of social issues, volunteering their time for fellow students or supporting charities the way teens are today. And, honestly, I'm not sure how well we're meeting these ideals as adults, either. I'm not saying teens have it all figured out but I don't think they get enough credit for managing everything thrown at them and doing so with such resiliency.

Teens are living through an era where pictures, videos, comments and even private moments are being scrutinized and to make it worse, the internet is forever. Think back to your most cringeworthy behaviors in high school and college. If you were unlucky enough to have incriminating photos or pictures taken from those events by someone's handheld point-and-shoot camera, they are at best lost altogether or at worst forgotten in a box collecting dust in an old friend's basement. Heck, I'm still close with my middle and high school best friends for insurance purposes.

Our kids are at the mercy of a single screen tap that would share their most embarrassing moments with the world. And it all happens in real time. When I was in school- which feels like two minutes ago but was actually two decades ago- I wouldn't know I missed a party or wasn't invited somewhere along with my friends until the next week, if at all. Now our children are subject to immediate and very public doses of rejection. As social creatures who are in a period of their life when social connection and stature are at peak importance and influence, this is a terribly painful reality.

In a best case scenario, teens are fortunate enough to focus on school and their future. Being in such a healthy and safe position to do so now means that on top of other stressors, they are being asked to juggle increasingly demanding schoolwork with building a resume for college through extracurricular activities, work and volunteerism. Academic standings are sent out reminding them of how they measure up, test score expectations are well-publicized and the message of "there's a college for everyone" competes with charts telling teens which ones probably won't want them.

Let's add on the pressure of building a resume for themselves through extracurriculars. Children and their families are taking on employment-level time commitments to these activities and for what? For bragging rights, a better college resume or a potential scholarship? It is a wonderful feeling to be accepted to the college of your dreams or to earn a scholarship, but what is the cost of pushing our children to such extremes to meet a societal ideal?

Even in the best of circumstances when teens are doing exactly what we hope they'll do, they are experiencing an extreme level of social, academic and extracurricular pressure. Oh, and let's not forget they lived through a PANDEMIC. Yes, I'm shouting! According to research released by the CDC in March 2022, high school students' reports of persistent feelings of sadness or hopelessness increased from 36.7% in 2019 to 44.2% in 2022.[30]

The pandemic most certainly stressed systems and added a layer of adversity for us as individuals, but it isn't the full picture of why we're in a mental health crisis on a national level. Our current epidemic of teen mental illness is not only related to the challenges teens faced during the pandemic, but the level of stress, expectation and social comparison they face on a daily basis within our culture. Because of the many pressures our teens face, the rates of teen sadness and depression have been steadily increasing since 2009 - a decade prior to COVID-19.[31]

As we dive into communicating with teens about the challenges they face including mental health and drug use, it is helpful to consider how their world is different from the one we grew up in. What is being asked or expected of them? What social or emotional challenges do they face? Because we look through the lens of our own experience, our expectations of their attitudes, behavior and relative success might not be realistic. The possible differences between our upbringing and the circumstances in which our children were raised are varied. And how positively or negatively these differences impact their well-being and decision-making is unique to each individual.

For example, if you were raised in a household or culture that gave teens a high level of responsibility within the family due to financial needs and you provide your child with a comfortable lifestyle, they may not value responsibility the way you do. If you were raised in an unpredictable environment and provide your children with safety and consistency, your children may not grasp or appreciate the stability you work so hard to maintain.

The point is, you may have had your own struggles and they may have been significant - even traumatic - but as my dear friend, Maria, says, "This isn't the Comparison Olympics". It is by and large unhelpful to expect that our children will view and engage with the world the way we did as young people. They are playing the hand they're dealt, and it may be a REALLY good one, but it's the only one they know. If we view their situation from our perspective, then what we've really done is lost perspective altogether. Let's base our approach to supporting our children on **empathy** for their experience, rather than living in our own past.

An understandable mistake parents make when trying to empathize is to compare their child's feelings in a given situation with their feelings in the same situation when they were young. For example, trying to compare how you felt when you weren't invited to a party compared to how they're feeling when not being invited. This is not empathy. Empathy is connecting with your child's emotion based on an experience you have had in which you felt that same way. Instead of matching your circumstance to theirs, the goal is to match your feeling to theirs.

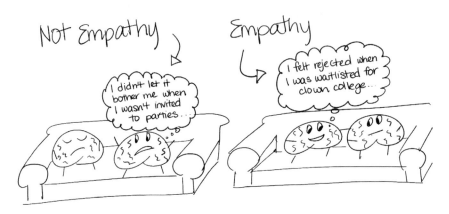

Being empathetic by matching your feeling to your child's feeling has several benefits. First, naming your own feelings and identifying theirs helps your child to learn how to name their own feelings. Naming feelings is an often-underestimated skill, but it is essential for healthy coping. In his best-selling book, The Whole-Brain Child, Dr. Dan Siegel uses the phrase "name to tame," to highlight that naming our feelings allows our brain to make the shift into emotional regulation so we can "tame" them.[32]

Empathy is not only important for parent-child relationships, it's important for all relationships. It is the foundation of healthy, supportive interactions whether they be within a family, friendship or romantic relationship. When we approach our kids with empathy, we are also modeling how they can use this skill with other people and allowing them to experience what others will feel when they do so.

Most importantly, empathy helps to increase your connection with your child. Harvard's Making Caring Common Project says, "when we empathize with our children they develop trusting, secure attachments with us."[33] From here, anything and everything you say increases in value because your child knows that you are able to understand and connect to their experience rather than making judgments or assumptions. Through empathic connection, you will be able to engage in open, honest dialogue and provide a compassionate sounding board for them to share their experiences and seek guidance.

Engaging through empathy is so effective it's almost cheating when it comes to improving your relationship with your child. Although I beg you to keep reading, if you were to stop here and only increase your practice of empathy with your children, you will have made leaps and bounds toward tackling any type of tough conversation, including conversations about drug use.

chapter nineteen

GET THE FACTS

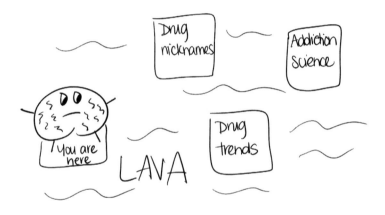

THE FLOOR IS LAVA & THE COUCH CUSHIONS ARE CON-
stantly moving. New lab-created drugs emerge constantly. Different substances go in and out of style. Teens' attitudes toward certain drugs change
and new versions of well-known drugs emerge. We are also learning more and
more about how the brain works and how problematic substance use affects a
variety of neurological processes. It can be intimidating and overwhelming to
try to stay on top of it, but you don't have to be an expert on this subject - your
job is to be an expert on your child.

Specialists in substance use prevention and treatment will tell you it
can be a challenge even for them to keep up with the evolution of trends and

developments in addiction science. Trends vary by age group, socioeconomic group, city, county, region and school. Our understanding of the brain and the impact of substance use on adolescent brain development is evolving constantly. Although professionals have an advantage, there are a myriad of opportunities available to parents to stay educated.

News or social media outlets are often the most accessible way to keep up with current trends. These outlets play a valuable role in helping information reach people quickly as it becomes available, but journalists are not experts nor are they necessarily thorough in their investigation into a particular topic. News cycles happen at the speed of sound, which can help raise the alarm but doesn't put journalists in a position to synthesize information with accuracy.

This doesn't mean that when we hear something through social or news media, we should ignore it. But we need facts without agendas. So, how will you know what to spend sleepless nights worrying about? The internet is here to help!

Web-based resources are ideal because they are updated regularly as new information becomes available. The following addiction science organizations are non-biased and evidence-based and are created by professionals who solely focus on the prevention and treatment of substance abuse. I visit their websites often to take advantage of their hard work researching and providing public products. Not only do they provide the in-depth research I nerd out on, they also have great resources for parents and teens:

- National Institute on Drug Abuse (NIDA) - *A division of the National Institutes on Health, NIDA performs extensive research on the topic of substance use and addiction. They provide information tailored to teens, caregivers and educators. NIDA partners with the University of Michigan to conduct the Monitoring the Future Survey which provides annual updates on youth substance use behaviors.*

- Centers for Disease Control and Prevention (CDC) - *Within the Department of Health & Human Services, the CDC is a "science-based, data-driven, service organization that protects the public's health."*[34] *The Be Tobacco Free webpage provides updated research and reports on youth tobacco use, public health campaigns and cessation tools. Their annual National Youth Tobacco Survey provides data on trends in teen use of nicotine products.*

- Substance Abuse and Mental Health Services Administration (SAMHSA) - *Agency within the U.S. Department of Health & Human Services. "SAMHSA provides leadership, supports programs and services, and devotes resources to helping the United States act on the knowledge that behavioral health is essential to health, prevention works, treatment is effective, and people recover."*[35] *The Public Messages section of their website provides information and videos for the general public.*

- Truth Initiative - *America's largest nonprofit public health organization focused on reducing tobacco and nicotine use. Truth Initiative conducts research, produces public health campaigns, advocates for policy change, supports community engagement programs and develops nicotine cessation programming. Their website provides a wealth of information on trends and resources for teens and parents.*

- Drug Enforcement Administration (DEA) - *The DEA offers drug information, data and informational resources for the public to aid in informed awareness and prevention. They also sponsor prescription drug take-back events to facilitate safe disposal of medications.*

While these are some of the most reputable sources of information, there are a variety of other organizations and educational institutions that are valuable sources of research and information. In general, educational institutions and public agencies conducting research are ideal sources of information. Non-profit organizations, public mental health agencies, prevention coalitions and academic institutions may also provide information, resources and support within your community. Your local school district may also employ Substance Abuse Prevention Specialists or Student Assistance Specialists who provide education and support to parents and students alike with the goal of reducing youth substance use.

I recommend checking in with these public organizations and institutions in your area about availability of workshops, parent seminars or other educational opportunities geared toward parents. These locally based opportunities can be incredibly valuable as they can provide a more tailored look at substance use in your community as well as personalized support.

chapter twenty

EVERYONE REMAIN CALM

WHEN GIVING PRESENTATIONS TO ADULTS ABOUT NAV-igating difficult interactions, I often ask the audience to humor me in creating a list of ways to escalate a situation out of control. With a lot of laughing and commentary, that list usually turns out to look something like this:

- *Tell someone to calm down*

- *Call someone names*

- *Embarrass/shame/mock the other person*

- *Yell/scream/use bad language*

- *Be physically aggressive*

Telling someone to calm down or some other condescending and invalidating comment just about always makes the list along with the other incendiary behaviors. Telling someone to calm down is not only unhelpful, dismissive and disrespectful it's also frustratingly non-specific.

Our idea of what is considered calm or upset is based on cultural expectations, interpretations of events and comfort level with emotion. What is considered an acceptable or rational display of emotion in one culture or family system may be very different from what is considered acceptable or rational in another. We really aren't in a position to tell someone else whether they're calm or not because we aren't working with the same definition of calm.

Personality also plays a role in the way we express ourselves when we feel passionately about something. Someone might be more expressive or reserved than another. Because of this wide range of what may or may not be considered "calm", saying "remain calm" is frustratingly nonspecific. And honestly, how can we as parents be expected to remain calm when faced with an issue as terrifying and risky as teen drug use?

So, as we prepare for these conversations with our teens about substance use, let's redefine what it means to remain calm. "Remain calm" should really be restated as "remain in control of yourself". We may be more or less animated, especially when we are passionate about something, but we all know when we are or are not in control of ourselves. When we lose control of ourselves, no matter what that threshold may be, our children will focus primarily on our lack of self-control and emotion and not the content of what we're saying. (Not connection before content again?!?) If we want to make an impact and be taken seriously, we need to remain in control - whatever that looks like for us.

Maintaining control of yourself will be easier if you have laid the foundation by having early conversations, imparting information over time and making clear what will happen if your child begins using. The planning, clarity, consistency and predictability you have invested in will be your ally. Even if you have not been setting this stage to date, here are a few tips for helping you remain in control of yourself:

- *Plan to have the conversation when all parties are ready*

- *Set your intention for what you want to say*

- *Check in with someone else about your plan to consider how you will respond to different viewpoints/outcomes*

- *Process emotional reactions with other adults beforehand and practice self-care*

- *Know your triggers and make a plan to take a break if needed and come back to the conversation when ready*

chapter twenty-one

TAKE ADVANTAGE OF
TEACHABLE MOMENTS

REPETITION CAN BE ANNOYING, BUT PREDICTABILITY is safety. Especially during the teen years, we can feel as though we're walking on eggshells trying not to encounter the dreaded eye roll and accompanying groans of "You already said that." If we want our kids to internalize healthy messages about substance use, we are going to have to repeat ourselves. Repetition really is essential for learning, but repeating ourselves on purpose to teens and pre-teens is a risky proposition.

As we attempt to tiptoe around teens' extra-sensitive nervous systems, we can use the power of **teachable moments** to sneak into their psyche, drop a nugget of wisdom and sneak back out without them catching on. Teachable moments are golden opportunities to be inconspicuous about telling someone how smart you are, giving your opinion or setting expectations. They are also valuable learning opportunities.

Teachable moments present themselves almost constantly if you're looking for them. They are real-life moments that provide a springboard for discussion about a particular topic. It could be something you see walking down the street, something you watch on tv, an event you reflect on - anything that you can connect to an important topic or make an example out of.

In our case a teachable moment allows us to deliver health-focused information about substance use or to make clear the rules and responses related to substance use in our home. You will want to keep these educational detours short by focusing on one or two pieces of information and then move on. A teachable moment is not a teachable hour or it would be called that, so keep it snappy and impart a small amount of wisdom without launching into a sermon. If you go on too long, you're likely to be met with resistance in the future as your child anticipates every one of these situations will turn into an exhaustive review of what you know.

Teachable moments are also an opportunity to set your expectations and make clear to your child what will happen if they cross the line. For example, starting middle school or high school is a great teachable moment about what new challenges they may encounter and how you expect them to handle it. This is not a one-time conversation. This is an ongoing check-in with your child about what they encounter in their environment and how prepared they are to handle those decisions.

If possible, teachable moments shouldn't feel too forced. You may feel this way early on as you're becoming more comfortable with discussions about substance use, but that will get easier over time. As you get used to having these conversations, please don't feel that you have to take advantage of literally every opportunity that crosses your path. In fact, by picking and choosing your "moment," you may just open the door for your child to make observations or share information they find relevant to what is in front of them. They may just turn the tables and provide you with a teachable moment of your own.

chapter twenty-two

FOCUS ON HEALTH

EARLY SUBSTANCE USE HAS MAJOR IMPLICATIONS FOR our children's brain development, experience of mental illness, and a variety of life outcomes. Our overall well-being can play an important role in protecting us or placing us at risk of substance use and if we begin using, our physical and mental health are profoundly impacted. Our conversations with teens must center around this dynamic interaction so they can think critically about substance use and their health.

I am asked constantly by teens about my position on legalization of marijuana or on alcohol and drug laws in general and I always respond the same: it doesn't make much difference to me either way. Regardless of what the law says, we all have an individual, personal choice to make about our own health. Laws change, politicians have agendas, political action committees have influence and money ultimately finds its ways into these decisions. In the current climate, we cannot assume that political decision-making is holding our best interest. It is not based on science. If it was, the legal age for use of any psychoactive substance would be 26; when the brain is fully developed and we are much less vulnerable.

Companies can try to sell us highly addictive nicotine products, but it is our choice to use them. Lawmakers can legalize marijuana recreationally at age 21 and we can still decide that we want to jumpstart our careers and wait for our brain to fully develop. While the law does send a message to us about what is socially acceptable and creates a perception of lower risk, it isn't the defining factor in our decision-making. No matter what the law says, we have the power of personal choice.

From a critical thinking perspective, it isn't reliable to focus on laws because laws are constantly changing and are completely subjective. And our teens know it. They know that other states and countries have different ways of handling this issue and this makes rules seem arbitrary and baseless. Remember that the teen brain hasn't fully developed in the area that anticipates future consequences, so the potential of having legal problems at some point in the future is not an immediate enough deterrent. And while they may be wary of police presence when engaging in use, their focus is on outsmarting them or hiding their use better, which misses the point by a mile.

Focusing on use as a moral or religious issue is another argument that can be seen by teens as subjective and is a difficult way to guide behavior unless the teen is fully connected to and engaged with this belief system. Morality and religion are interpreted differently by different people and teens are developing their own belief system and sense of the world around them. If your teen does subscribe to your moral and/or religious views, then this could be valuable for them. If they do not, focusing on them as a way of trying to deter your child will likely only create conflict and frustration.

At the end of the day, we are worried about their physical, emotional and spiritual health and those are immediately impacted by using. So that is where our energy must go. To keep our conversations health-focused, we should incorporate the following information:

- *Addiction is a brain disease which begins with chosen behavior but becomes compulsive and gets worse over time (increasing symptoms, health problems and consequences). While people do recover, addiction does not improve on its own.*
- *The adolescent brain is still developing and is more easily changed by substance use. Addiction develops much faster for young people.*

- *Drug use makes mental health problems worse.*

- *Drug use can cause mental illness to develop.*

- *Drug use impairs healthy brain development.*

- *Everyone's risk of problematic substance use is unique - refer back to Part II to review what these risk factors are.*

- *Encourage discussion with people who have knowledge about substance use. Hearing from multiple trustworthy sources reinforces the information and keeps the focus on the facts.*

chapter twenty-three

REDUCE SHAME

ARGUABLY TODAY'S MOST FAMOUS SHAME AND VUL-
nerability researcher, Dr. Brené Brown, has been shouting from the rooftops
that shame negatively impacts our well-being and blocks our ability to be
vulnerable and connect with others. As we try to break free from the shame
and stigma associated with substance use, her work offers valuable guidance.

In an interview on Oprah's Super Soul Sunday podcast, Dr. Brown
described that "Shame [is] highly correlated with addiction, depression, eat-
ing disorders, violence, bullying and aggression. Guilt? Inversely correlated
with those." She explains that this difference has to do with the fact that guilt
focuses on behavior while shame focuses on self.[36]

Guilt gives us direction. It tells us that a behavior is wrong and that
wrong can be corrected. Shame, on the other hand, is deeply felt and personal.
According to the Gottman Institute, **toxic shame** "can be very harmful psychologically. It's deeply absorbed in the nervous system. . . [and] leads to feeling
alone, disconnected, and more likely to engage in self-destructive behaviors."[37]

When we weaponize shame with threats about ostracizing, discon-
necting and/or disowning, it becomes toxic. Toxic shame keeps people from
doing the one thing that can get them where they need to be - asking for help.
Asking for help requires vulnerability and is a challenge even under the best

READ THIS AND CALL ME IN THE MORNING

circumstances. People avoid letting others in out of fear of rejection and this avoidance only continues to grow as the situation becomes more severe. Acknowledging unmanageable drug use can be so crushingly embarrassing and shameful that many people try in vain to figure it out alone or give up trying altogether.

"Vulnerability is not winning or losing; it's having the courage to show up and be seen when we have no control over the outcome."[38]

-Excerpt from Rising Strong by Brene Brown, Ph.D., MSW

For some, the vulnerability needed to take steps toward health, recovery or treatment comes not as a choice but out of utter desperation. This is what you have likely heard referred to as "rock bottom". This term refers to a moment where someone is finally ready to get help when things get bad enough. It is, in part, due to the unavoidable vulnerability caused by tragic circumstances.

But how impossible would it feel to be told that you have to wait for "rock bottom?" Or that you have to wait for your child to experience extreme, painful consequences in order to turn things around? I hope you're shaking your head with a clear "absolutely not." Help can happen at any stage in this process and is more easily accessed by someone who feels safe enough to be vulnerable.

Kids ask for help in lots of ways well before they've reached the point of problematic drug use. Early on they need help with answers to questions about difficult topics. Later they might need help getting out of an uncomfortable or risky situation. These early opportunities and others like them set the tone for how we respond to help-seeking and vulnerability in our household.

If we aim to invite our children into connection and provide them a safe space for change, we're going to need some handy-dandy strategies for reducing shame. In line with Dr. Brown's description of the benefits guilt, the Gottman Institute says, "Healthy shame guides toward self-correction, making amends, and growth."[39] What healthy shame and guilt have in common is a focus on correcting behavior and repairing connection. Wait a minute - are we talking about connection again?! The two strategies I'd like to suggest align with these ideas of healthy shame and guilt and keep the focus on behavior.

Noticing

Noticing involves pointing out behaviors or outcomes without assigning a value judgment to it. The focus stays on what the person is doing, not on how we interpret or perceive them as a result. Noticing removes the patterns of judgment and shame we can often get drawn into. For example:

"That's a good drawing!" (value judgment)
VS
"I see you are putting a lot of effort into that drawing" (noticing)

Although "good drawing" is a positive judgment, it is a judgment nonetheless and implies that the judgment could've gone either way. It sends an unintended message that next time it might not be a good drawing or might not earn our praise. Noticing allows us to instead highlight that we are attending to our child's behaviors without making any assessment of it. The behavior can stand alone and we are not involving ourselves to judge. We are present with them and interested in what they do and how they feel.

Don't get me wrong - you can still tell your children how proud you are and congratulate them on their successes. Sometimes it is even necessary to make judgments or assessments of behavior. The key is not to focus so heavily on good/bad interpretations that you set your child up to expect that you will assign a judgment to every circumstance.

It is easy to see how assigning negative judgments to things can foster shame, but **overvaluation** can be harmful to children as well. Overvaluation involves repeatedly assigning an undeserved high value to your child's character or behavior. Doing so can lead to unhealthy development and contribute to narcissistic attitudes and behaviors. Brummelman, et al. found that "Narcissism was predicted by parental overvaluation." Self-esteem, on the other hand, "was predicted by parental warmth… children come to see themselves as they believe to be seen by significant others, as if they learn to see themselves through others' eyes."[40] Avoiding the use of excessive judgment with simple noticing will help foster healthy self-esteem and reduce shame.

Separating the person from the problem

Taking nonjudgmental noticing one step further, therapists practice distancing the person from the problem when discussing unhealthy behaviors. The person is not the problem, the problem is the problem. We identify the behavior as a point of discussion separate from the person's sense of self. This allows both the therapist and the person to examine the problem and any possible solutions. This eases tension and increases engagement in problem-solving.

This does not nullify personal responsibility or discount the consequences of the behavior. In fact, it emphasizes accountability and accountability is protective. This helps the person make an even stronger connection to the behavior and its consequences and increase a sense of choice-making about the behavior. It can help someone shift from "I keep getting in trouble because I'm a bad person" to "I keep getting in trouble because of disrespectful behavior." Now the disrespectful behavior is the problem, which is a problem that can be solved.

Sometimes a behavior is morally wrong, harmful or just plain stupid and value judgments might be accurate. But if we are to make a shame-free safe space for our kids, then we will at some point have to choose between being right and being helpful. Being right is easy, especially as a parent with a great deal of life experience. Those experiences and a fully developed brain allow you to anticipate outcomes and think rationally. But bragging about your superior prefrontal cortex isn't going to do you or your child any favors. Sometimes we have to swallow our pride and abandon being right in order to be helpful.

Your child is listening carefully to everything you say and how you say it, especially when you don't want them to. Choosing words carefully, not making things personal and reducing your use of value judgments will set the stage for vulnerability and help-seeking. Your child will know that they don't have to choose between honesty and your affection.

Shame checklist:

- *Notice behavior and their outcomes without assigning value judgments*
- *Separate the problem behavior from the person*
- *Reinforce vulnerability as a healthy step toward help-seeking*
- *Offer a way to correct the behavior and focus on solutions*

chapter twenty-four

THE POWER OF "AND"

AS A PARENT, HOW WOULD YOU FEEL IF SOMEONE said, "You are a great parent BUT your child has a problem with drug use"? I'd venture a guess that you might feel the way I would - that my child's drug use somehow negates or casts doubt on my ability to parent. Or that my parenting wasn't good enough to protect my child from substance use.

Author and relationship coach Michael S. Sorensen writes that "when used to connect two phrases in a sentence, the word "but" essentially dismisses the first phrase altogether. This isn't always an issue, but when it undoes praise, agreement, or an important point, it can start to become a problem."[41] Stereotypes and unconscious biases are evident when we make statements like "he's a good kid but he's got a serious problem" instead of "he's a good kid and he's got a serious problem." I have many times been told by someone "oh, she's not using, she's a good kid." I bet you know me well enough by now to expect that this is another one of those shoe-throwing triggers for me.

In therapy we promote a **"both-and"** perspective to help people acknowledge and accept that two seemingly opposite ideas can be true. When we view things in this way, we recognize that life is complex. It is not a series of black and white, this or that possibilities, especially when people are involved. Life can be both beautiful and heart-breaking. Food can be both healthy and delicious (hard to believe, I know!). And people can be both lovable and flawed. We can love and respect people for their strengths and successes and acknowledge unhealthy and/or destructive behaviors.

Viewing people who use alcohol and other drugs with a "both-and" perspective will help you maintain a non-judgmental stance and reduce your own bias and stigma toward people suffering with the disease of addiction. This small change in the way we talk also prepares us to acknowledge the possibility of our own, beloved child using and will help us more accurately recognize any warning signs of use if they arise. This shift in perspective forms the foundation for approaching people who struggle with substance use with both love and accountability.

As you approach these discussions with your children, keep this idea of both-and in mind. It will help you avoid judgment, focus on health and avoid enabling. Below are some examples of how you can use both-and with your child:

*"You are smart **and** you made unsafe decisions"*
*"I love you **and** I will not accept this behavior."*
*"I accept your apology **and** your behavior has consequences."*
*"I want to trust you **and** trust takes time to build."*
*"You are a kind, loving person **and** this behavior is manipulative."*

PART IV: WAIVE THE RED FLAG

IDEALLY, OUR NEW-FOUND KNOWLEDGE AND STRATE-gies for prevention will help us raise educated kids who think critically about substance use and seek support when they need it. But because we don't control outcomes, we need to be prepared to intervene if early signs of substance use arise. In this section we will discuss how to identify warning signs of substance use and how to rule out substance use as a contributing factor to challenges and changes in our teens' lives.

chapter twenty-five

THE WARNING SIGNS

MOST PARENTS ARE SURE THEIR CHILD ISN'T USING when confronted with concerns about their well-being. I have been on the other end of many of these conversations. So often I have finished an evaluation with a teen who shared honestly about their substance use and then had to discuss the assessment results with a parent who came in sure that this wasn't possible. Because of our bias and vested interest in disbelieving the possibility of substance use, we might not be in the best position as parents to make a quick judgment call about whether substance use is contributing to the problems our teens are facing.

Teens grow and change but they don't develop entirely new personality traits, goals, relationships, etc. overnight. By "overnight" I mean a period of several weeks to several months - the length of time it can take for substance use to cause problematic changes to the teen brain. If we chip away at our unconscious bias about substance use and familiarize ourselves with what teen substance use really looks like, we will be more likely to catch emerging problems early on and prevent things from getting worse. Substance use escalates so quickly for our teens that addressing this issue early can very literally save them from years of hardship.

The stereotypes we have about people with substance use problems generally involve a few themes: homelessness, crime, physical ailments, changes to appearance and financial failure. We discussed in our chapter titled Checking your bias, that teen substance use doesn't always fit these stereotypes. Most teens aren't expected to hold a job or keep a roof over their own head. They have a variety of people in their lives available to support them and help keep things afloat. So, what does it look like when kids are using?

Drug use alters the brain's development and functioning, causing predictable changes to the way people think, feel and behave. Involvement in the drug culture also brings about common changes to the way young people relate to others and engage with their environment. Individually, these symptoms are not necessarily indicators of substance use, but if you see multiple symptoms together and especially if you find your child in possession of drugs or paraphernalia, a deeper investigation into the prevalence of their drug use is warranted.

Each of the symptoms below are commonly associated with substance use in the teen years. These symptoms are the natural result of the biological and social changes caused by substance use and the culture around it, which is why they appear so typically for people who use regularly. I am including a brief description of how or why these symptoms occur so we can see how these puzzle pieces fit together.

Changes in friend group and associating with using peers - Spending more and more time using means spending more and more time with people who use or who condone using. It also means distancing from friends who object to this decision or who are seen as judging other friendships and choices. Often, what teens perceive as judgmental is really legitimate concern on the part of loved ones who recognize unhealthy changes.

Mood instability - Teens are working with a brain that is essentially under construction. Their emotional control center is still in the process of developing toward healthy functioning. Adding substance use to this mix makes for heightened emotions and a slowing down of activity in this area of the brain. A teen who is using will likely present as depressed, anxious and with attention and learning difficulties. Some teens, especially those using marijuana or other hallucinogenic drugs may experience psychotic symptoms as well. (See Chapter 9: Mental Illness and Trauma for more information).

Loss of motivation or interest in activities - The impact of drug use on the natural production of Dopamine (our value & reward chemical) leads the brain to place higher value and anticipated reward on the drug than other things. Therefore, our desire to engage in other activities goes down, which we experience as lack of motivation. Due to the damage caused to our dopamine receptors, we are also unable to experience the same reward from activities we used to enjoy. The drug is increasingly the priority and other previously important pursuits are cast aside or are no match for the biochemical enjoyment the drug gives.

Irritability and/or increased conflict with others - Substance use can increase feelings of irritability, leading to increased conflict with others, especially those who are interfering with their lifestyle. Perceptions are altered as well, which can lead to inaccurate interpretation of others' behavior, words or intentions. Undesirable behaviors like sneaking out, skipping class, avoiding schoolwork, etc., can lead to consequences and conflict with authority figures or peers. Teens who are using substances will struggle to navigate conflict effectively.

Isolation/withdrawing from family and/or friends - Especially when it is clear that substance use will be frowned upon, teens distance themselves from those who disapprove. This helps them to use without detection, conflict or consequences but it also leads to disconnection from others.

Money or items unaccounted for - Teens are initially able to use for free by using small amounts in a group setting where others are using more heavily. As they use more regularly they might buy food for others as payment or trade items of value to obtain drugs. As their use escalates, they may sell valuable items or begin selling the drug itself in order to support their use.

Decline in grades - A constellation of different issues related to substance use can impact academic performance. Although different drugs impact the brain differently, many of them affect our brain's motivation for non-drug-related activities and our ability to pay attention and to learn. The lifestyle of using drugs does not encourage or allow much time to do schoolwork. The lack of motivation accompanying substance use makes their academic workload daunting and can leave kids feeling overwhelmed by what others might consider manageable tasks.

Seemingly unfazed by consequences - As substance use increases, the dopamine reward process that occurs in the brain can overshadow consequences experienced later on. They may not respond to common consequences like taking the phone away or being grounded so you may have to get creative with your responses. To protect their highly valued drug use, they are likely to use defense mechanisms like minimizing or rationalizing away any natural or logical consequences. Consequences paired with supportive intervention can make a positive impact, but it takes a coordinated and consistent effort.

Illegal activity/violating previously held values/morals - To some extent illegal activity is a requirement of using. Nowhere is substance use legal for young people, although it is not necessarily a criminal offense in all states. The changes in their brain, their peer connections and their environments associated with the drug culture increase the likelihood that teens who are using will engage in risky behavior. People under the influence are more likely to act impulsively and engage in behavior they otherwise wouldn't, including violent behavior. A 2018 study found that binge-drinking, sedatives and cannabis use were correlated with higher rates of violent crime.[42]

Lying and manipulation - This is also somewhat a requirement of using. Dishonesty about behavior, misdirection about warning signs and manipulation in order to get what they want are necessary elements of maintaining regular substance use. If your child is lying to you it may be a function of their drug use rather than an indication that you haven't instilled appropriate values in them. Many of the teens I work with feel ashamed about lying but continue to do so in order to avoid conflict, stress or discovery.

If we look at lying as a symptom of their use, we can more easily see that our children's behavior is not a personal affront or assault on our relationship with them, but a desperate effort to maintain the double-life they're living.

Whereabouts unaccounted for - Teens who are using tend to do so in other people's homes or in public areas like parks, wooded areas or shopping centers. Since most parents don't want their children roaming around in undefined areas or unknown households, teens often lie about where they're going or who they're with. Verifying your child's location with apps or contact with other parents can help you make sure your child's whereabouts are accounted for. (And if your child tells you, "No one's parents have to talk to other people's parents," you heard it here first - that's not true).

Possession of drugs or paraphernalia - According to a 2011 study, possession of paraphernalia is the single largest indicator of substance use.[43] If you find your child in possession of drugs or items that are involved in using drugs, trust me when I say they are not holding it for a friend. Trying something for the first time or using occasionally when presented with the opportunity does not typically cause someone to keep drugs or paraphernalia in their possession.

I can't stress enough how quickly the above changes can happen for young people. I have worked with teens who start using regularly during the summer and by Thanksgiving things have gone dramatically downhill. Their grades are severely impacted, they have little motivation for things they used to enjoy, and they are experiencing consequences in school and at home. Most interestingly, rarely does anyone in their life attribute these changes to drug use.

Although the social, emotional and behavioral changes that stem from regular substance use are predictable, they can masquerade as other issues like learning disabilities, mental illness and relationship problems, among others. Looking from the outside, adults see these symptoms and quickly assign the most comfortable explanation. By this I mean that we find an explanation that feels somewhat safer or more familiar to us and that we believe gives us a clear path to a resolution.

In many cases the simplest answer tends to be the right one, but in this case the simplest answer (drug use) isn't the most favorable. A child who has trouble concentrating, low mood, is withdrawn and irritable and reports suicidal thoughts is not necessarily a depressed child. They certainly could be, but this is a common presentation for a child with a substance use problem, especially one whose symptoms came on suddenly. I have seen this play out a number of times and here is how that scenario unfolds:

Parent seeks therapy for supposedly depressed child. Child denies or minimizes their substance because they, too, want the problem to be anything other than drug use. Therapist agrees child is depressed. The child gradually discloses substance use and the therapist buys into the idea that the child is "self-medicating." (Eye roll emoji) Despite having a great therapist and maybe even enjoying going to therapy, the symptoms persist and their drug use escalates.

These stories are much more common than you might think. So common, in fact, that I am writing this book hoping to save parents from this same fate. I have been involved in many situations in which people try to apply an academic or mental health solution to a substance abuse problem with little to no results. This happens with teens using everything from nicotine to PCP and presenting with what is mistaken for anything from a learning disability to a psychotic disorder.

Well-meaning people see symptoms that match a particular issue and assume they've found an explanation. No need to ask any further, right? Then, frustratingly, the intervention that should match doesn't work. So, they try another one and then another until they decide that the child just isn't trying hard enough or maybe there is another mental health or academic problem in the way and then layer interventions on top.

If we aren't willing to even look at the possibility that substance use has led our child down this path, we are going to walk a long way down the wrong one looking for a solution. I have seen the frustration and hopelessness this can cause, but it doesn't have to. If ruling out substance use becomes a standard part of our decision-making process, we can save valuable time, money and energy. We can also drastically improve outcomes for those kids who spend years being misdiagnosed and struggling due to unmet needs.

I would like to scream from the rooftops that:

If we know that experimenting with substance use during teen years
is common
AND
We know that substance use escalates quickly for young people
AND
We know that substance use changes the way people think, feel and behave
THEN
We should first consider drug use as a possible source of our child's academic,
mental health or behavioral difficulty

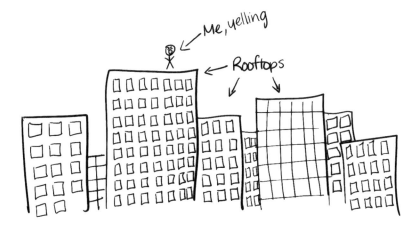

Now that we are committing to keeping our eyes open for potential symptoms of drug use and taking steps to avoid misdiagnosis, how are we going to know what's what? In therapy, we call this ruling something out. Ruling out substance use means gathering information to determine whether or not substance use is contributing to the concerns we see. Without further ado, let's move along to the next chapter and learn about ruling out substance use.

chapter twenty-six

RULING IT OUT

RULING OUT SUBSTANCE USE INVOLVES GATHERING A variety of information from multiple sources. In order to determine if substance use could be contributing to any social, emotional, physical or cognitive symptoms a person is experiencing, we will need to take a wide range of information into account. In this chapter we will review how a substance use specialist would go about ruling substance use in or out. Who you involve in gathering this information or making this determination is up to you, but I'm going to describe here how a substance use specialist would go about this. In my opinion, a full substance use evaluation is the gold standard in ruling out substance use and will shed some light on what you might consider if you are adamant you want to go this alone.

Drug testing

The most straightforward way to determine if someone is using a drug is with direct testing. Urine, blood, saliva or hair analysis can help obtain an objective picture of your child's substance use. All of these have their own benefits and drawbacks and although a positive test may confirm substance use, they aren't able to definitively rule out substance use altogether.

Urine screens tend to be the most widely used because they are cost-effective, accessible and can test for recent drug use with accuracy. Urine screening kits can be purchased over the counter or online from major retailers and can deliver results almost instantly. Instant test kits tend to be less effective and more likely to reveal a false negative result.

Urine screenings can be done at your physician's office, or directly through a laboratory service. These professional-grade analyses are able to screen for a wider variety of substances and with more precision. With any drug test, you will want to be clear with your doctor or lab technician which substances they are testing for so you will know what you are trying to rule in or out.

Saliva tests involve swabbing the mouth with a sponge or absorbent pad. Like urine screenings, these tests can be purchased as instant home testing kits or administered by a laboratory service. These are not as commonly used as urine tests but are preferred in certain settings because they can be more easily observed to ensure that the sample is authentic. The primary drawback to saliva testing is that it generally will only detect the presence of drug use within 5 to 48 hours after use.[44]

Blood testing is performed with a trained professional and results are provided by a laboratory. Like saliva, drug testing using a blood sample has a brief detection window, allowing for detection within minutes to hours of last use.[45] These are ideal if someone appears to be under the influence and you want to determine what drugs are in their system.

Hair testing is done using hair follicles and has a long detection window. Hair testing can help identify drug use occurring within the past several months or even years.[46] This can be done through a laboratory but home testing kits that allow you to mail the sample to a laboratory can also be purchased through a laboratory's website.

No matter which medical test you seek out, the test is only as good as the substance you test for. No test will allow you to identify the presence of every possible drug of abuse. Additionally, newer or less common drug compounds that a young person might abuse may not yet have a specific test available to identify them or the test may be very expensive. Mentioned previously but worth mentioning again, most drugs leave the body within hours to a few days and are therefore harder to detect on any random drug screening.

The variety of limitations inherent in drug testing amount to the fact that drug testing can be a helpful component of identifying drug use but should not be the end-all be-all for determining the presence of drug use. Other information will prove much more helpful. The most valuable use I've found for drug testing is not in the evaluation process but in providing accountability for someone with a known history of use. Providing ongoing random drug testing for a teen with a known history of use can be a helpful, tangible way for them to demonstrate progress with sobriety.

Standardized screening instruments

There are a variety of standardized assessments that can be given in different settings. These are questionnaires designed to flag attitudes, behaviors or symptoms that could demonstrate problematic substance use. Most are given in a physician's office or by trained mental health professionals.

Screening tools used in primary care settings are most often simpler and rely on the person to accurately report on their use. Assessment tools used by mental health professionals, especially those used by substance use specialists, are usually more in-depth and can even detect if a person is attempting to deceive the test. Standardized tests across these different settings have been shown to be effective at accurately identifying problematic substance use. If your child's results on one of these questionnaires indicates likelihood of problematic use, you'll want to take those results seriously.

Self-report

Wouldn't it be nice if teens would accurately self-report their substance use to whoever asks? Everyone's life would be a lot easier if this were this case, but until that day comes, we will need to account for the likelihood that our kids will not want to share this information openly. In some cases, teens may admit to one-time use or infrequent use to explain away evidence of use. I half-jokingly encourage parents to multiply whatever teens self-report by at least 3x to get a more accurate picture of their use.

This is another benefit of involving professionals or other trusted adults in the process of ruling out substance use. Sometimes it is easier for teens to be honest within an objective third party, especially if that person is expected to uphold confidentiality.

I am often amazed by the things teens will tell me even though they just met me. And generally speaking, what they tell me on day one isn't nearly as much as they'll tell me by their third visit. Encouraging your teen to talk openly with other adults or professionals can help you get to the heart of what is going on much faster.

Clinical interview

As a substance use counselor doing multiple substance use assessments each week, my goal was to gain as much of a holistic view of each person as possible before making any diagnosis or recommendations. This was one of the things I truly loved about my job - getting to know each person and how their unique life experiences, strengths and challenges have led them to where they are. I was able to take concrete information from drug testing, screenings and self-report and put it into context with the information I gained by completing a clinical interview.

In a clinical interview professionals ask teens about their physical health, relationships, mental health symptoms, academics, trauma history, activities and coping skills. This information allows them to make sense of the overall picture of someone's well-being and how substance use interacts with other factors. Essentially, they identify the person's unique risk factors, protective factors, mental health skills, support systems and symptoms of mental illness or substance use. By taking all of these factors into account, professionals are able to recognize patterns and symptoms consistent with substance use that may be missed by others.

The ability to pull together a variety of information and make an evaluation of the presence of any substance use in the context of someone's life is the major benefit of seeking out a full substance use evaluation with a trained professional. I know that even the mention of something like this can sound like a presumption of guilt, so to speak. But this is where the change needs to happen. If this is a health issue, our investigation is truly about determining whether our child is experiencing a health problem. And any evaluation is with the purpose of identifying a health need and seeking appropriate health care.

I can understand apprehension about seeking a substance use evaluation. An initial appointment with a mental health professional might be seen as a foregone conclusion that someone will enter treatment, but this is not the case. On many occasions I've met with teens and their families and ultimately came to the conclusion that treatment was not needed. Believe me, people who enter the counseling field, especially substance use counseling, don't do so for the money. If there is no indication of a substance use problem, a professional will be more than happy to make alternative recommendations for appropriate support.

Substance use therapists are uniquely positioned to provide these assessments and make these determinations. Someone who has spent significant amounts of time working directly with teens with substance use needs is in a better position to recognize language, attitudes and patterns of behavior that indicate drug use than others. Although I am admittedly biased, I hope that you will see their work as a specialty the way it deserves to be seen.

I want to acknowledge that in the area where I live and work, we have the privilege of a variety of mental health and substance abuse treatment services. In areas like this, seeking out a substance use specialist is a choice available to most. This may not be the case where you live, and you may not have the ability to be picky about the medical or mental health providers you meet with.

With the information you've gained about risk, symptoms and warning signs, I hope you feel more prepared to advocate for your child to receive quality assessment and care wherever you can find it. It is appropriate for you to ask any professional you meet with about their level of understanding and experience with substance use. An initial appointment is not only an opportunity for the professional to learn about your child and their needs, but also for you to determine if they are a good fit for your family.

In the next chapter we will explore what comes next if you have to move from evaluation to intervention.

chapter twenty-seven

EARLY INTERVENTION

OK, SO YOU KEPT YOUR EYES OPEN FOR WARNING signs and maybe even went the route of a formal substance use assessment and you've discovered that your teen is, in fact, using. What comes next? I'll answer this the way most teens like to answer difficult questions: "it depends." Frustrating, right?

If you are looking to go this on your own and intervene without any formalized treatment, you can fall back on all of the concepts we've discussed so far. You will just be incorporating them from a position of knowing your child is using rather than preparing for the possibility. Much of what we've talked about throughout this book in terms of talking to and supporting your kids are beneficial for supporting your child's well-being regardless of whether they've started using or not.

Increasing accountability, structure and supervision will help your teen make safe decisions and help you rebuild trust. Making expectations clear, setting limits & enforcing them will help them anticipate outcomes and reduce conflict. Avoiding shame and creating restorative opportunities for change will allow your child to see a clear path to health and healing. Providing education about drug use and its impact on brain health and development will help your child identify the impact their use has on different parts of their life and begin to invest in the recovery process. And of course, empathy will always help you navigate emotionally-charged situations and connect with your child.

Connection is the most important thing to focus on as you try to help your child get back on track. This is not the moment to blame others, shut down activities as a consequence or isolate your child and your family from the outside world. Get your child involved in healthy activities at school or in the community and foster connections with trusted adults. Rebuild your own connection with your teen by practicing that old empathy trick I've been so shamelessly plugging for the past 100 pages or so.

It can be incredibly frustrating and exhausting to deal with a teen who is using substances. Some of the warning signs we just reviewed like lying, manipulation, sneaking out and criminal behavior can lead to serious conflict and can make for deeply strained relationships. I've had parents in my office lamenting that their child isn't the person they once knew and teens who complain that their parents don't love them or who feel disconnected from their family altogether.

Rebuilding trust and connection after a period of broken trust and/or conflict surrounding substance use behaviors can be difficult, especially given that this change does not occur in a straight line. This is a process and both the change and healing we need takes time. Respecting the legitimacy of this as a health issue requires accepting that this recovery and healing process will not happen overnight. We didn't arrive at this point in our relationships overnight so we can't expect an immediate fix.

If you are in a position where you have discovered your child is using, this is likely new territory for you and definitely new territory in your relationship with that child. It puts you both in a position of needing to find a solution and to chart a course neither of you have taken. That may seem like an incredibly obvious course of action - just stop using - but the way to move forward in your relationship is less prescriptive.

However large or small this issue has become for your child, your goal as a parent working through this with them is to be **restorative**. Approaching a problem in a restorative way means honoring the impact on those involved, placing value on rebuilding the relationship and working toward a solution. Agreements are made about how to move forward, providing a clear path for each person to regain connection and make amends for any harm done.

Using a restorative approach with your child involves just about everything discussed in Part IV, including staying calm, reducing shame and judgment and, of course, empathy. These ideals for healthy communication don't suddenly get thrown out the window when we move from prevention to intervention. In fact, they are even more relevant under those conditions.

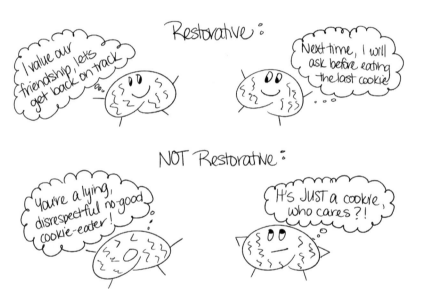

Building on a foundation of healthy communication, being restorative also means developing a clear path to rebuilding your relationship. Any goal requires clear action to complete and relationship goals are no different. What concrete behaviors and indicators will help you build trust? What will the process of regaining privileges look like? What agreements can you make about how you will spend time together to connect? What can be done to demonstrate the healthy change you are expecting to see? Clear next steps and commitment to getting back on track as a family will serve as a guidepost for your child's decision-making.

Depending on how much your relationship with your child has been impacted, you may need to do some of your own work to make yourself available to rebuilding trust and reconnecting with them. Seeking your own support from a therapist may help you set yourself up for success in these moments. Each person in a relationship has to take care of what's on their side of the fence (aka boundary) to be more successful in challenging interactions. Getting help on your end may be an important part of this change process.

When substance use is caught early on and symptoms are minimal, it can be appropriate to address this issue within your home. But there may come a time, if your child is experiencing more serious symptoms, that you will benefit much more from the support and guidance of a trained professional. In this case, an experienced treatment provider will help your family find the most effective path forward.

PART V:
FINAL THOUGHTS

I SAID IT BEFORE AND I'LL SAY IT AGAIN: WE'RE HERE for a good time, not a long time. Let's wrap it up.

chapter twenty-eight

PLEASE TAKE ONE ...

WE HAVE COVERED A LOT OF GROUND IN A SHORT amount of time. The more intricate details of these ideas and extensive research behind them are out there for you to dive into if you wish, but intricate and extensive is not the name of our game. We set out to gain an overview and to "get it" just enough to be preventative and aware of this issue. Got it? Good.

Although my college days are long behind me, I have a vivid memory of one of my psychology professors talking about the percentage of information we forget immediately after taking a test. Ironically, this is one of the few things I can remember about that class. Our brain is not designed to retain everything it takes in. It does its best to use cues about what's important and hold on to meaningful, useful information, but just like my shoe closet, there is only room for so much stuff. For easy reference and memory, here are some key takeaways from our journey together:

- *Substance use is a health issue, not a moral issue.*
- *All teens are at higher risk of problematic substance use due to their brain's high level of neuroplasticity.*
- *Teens with family history of addiction, mental illness and trauma, substance use in their environment and those who identify as LGBTQ+ are at even higher risk than others.*

- *Our brain is affected by drug use in predictable ways that may be misinterpreted as academic or mental health problems.*

- *To make conversations about substance use more effective, talk to your child early and often, remain calm, reduce shame and avoid scare tactics.*

- *Empathy is essential to building connections and improving communication.*

- *Accountability will help your child make healthier decisions and help you identify needs early.*

- *Ruling out substance use is an important first step toward identifying our child's true needs.*

- *If you notice warning signs of substance use, seek competent care from a professional skilled and experienced specifically in the realm of substance use treatment.*

chapter twenty-nine

QUICKSAND

I HAVE COME TO THINK OF SUBSTANCE USE AS QUICK-sand. Some teens avoid it completely and some quickly see a way around or out of it. Others fall into it and don't realize it's pulling them down until it's too late. And as they are pulled under, it is hard to see or hear the child you know and love. And for the child it gets darker and darker and increasingly impossible to see a way out, leaving them disconnected and helpless.

I hope you can walk away from reading this with an understanding that this quicksand is a legitimate hazard for all young people, not just a select few. And that addressing this issue early before our kids are in too deep will improve their likelihood of success.

Overcoming bias and disbelief to explore whether or not your child's use has surpassed average teenage experimentation is a brave and difficult step to take. It is much easier to rationalize away early warning signs and even easier to avoid this topic altogether.

When I give presentations, I am often preaching to the choir. Parents who are already utilizing the advice we share for preventing teen substance use tend to be the ones attending these presentations, asking questions and wondering if their child is having an issue. It is the parents who don't ask the questions that tend to find themselves in places they never imagined they'd be and are unprepared when they arrive.

Through awareness and open discussion, we can dramatically change the future landscape of teen substance use. Having healthy conversations with your child and encouraging them to have conversations with others is ultimately an act of societal change. We have created the culture of stigma and silence surrounding mental health and substance use and we all have a role to play in rebuilding it into something that allows our kids to seek help and change course early on.

We have taken a very boiled-down look at some incredibly important topics. I hope this lit a spark for you to be more aware and open about teen substance use. If you're still unsure what to do or how to support your child, continue seeking out information and guidance from professionals who can help you work through any roadblocks and create a plan tailored to your needs.

Now that we've come to the end of our time together, I challenge you to take what you've read and do something with it. I challenge you to spread this information and these ideas by sharing them in some form or another. Have conversations with your kids, talk to other parents, share information in your social circle or support prevention efforts in your community. Pay it forward by donating this book or giving it to someone else who definitely doesn't think this could be a problem for their perfect kid. Be the change, and all that jazz.

GLOSSARY

Accountability - accepting responsibility for the outcome of words and/or actions.

Addiction - American Society of Addiction Medicine defines addiction as "a treatable, chronic medical disease involving complex interactions among brain circuits, genetics, the environment, and an individual's life experiences. People with addiction use substances or engage in behaviors that become compulsive and often continue despite harmful consequences."[47]

"both-and" - acknowledging that more than one seemingly at-odds truth can exist simultaneously.

Cisgender - when a person's gender identity coincides with their sex assigned at birth.

Confirmation bias - "Once we have formed a view, we embrace information that confirms that view while ignoring, or rejecting, information that casts doubt on it."[48]

Co-occurring illness - presence of more than one medical condition. For our purposes, this refers to the presence of both a mental illness and substance use disorder.

Dopamine - neurotransmitter (aka chemical messenger in the brain) that is released when our brain experiences pleasure.

Emotional Thermostat - someone who is empowered to regulate their emotions regardless of external factors.

Emotional Thermometer - someone whose emotions are dictated by environmental stressors.

Empathy - identifying and connecting with another person's feelings.

Enabling - reinforcing a behavior by allowing someone to avoid consequences for their actions.

Epigenetics - changes to genetic material caused by environmental influences that affect the expression of our genes.[49]

Gateway Hypothesis - Dr. Denise Kandel's observations about a pattern of escalating substance use beginning with nicotine, alcohol and marijuana use.

Limbic system - a collection of structures in the brain that control emotion, memory, arousal, learning and reward, among other functions.

Mental Health - "Mental health is a state of mental well-being that enables people to cope with the stresses of life, realize their abilities, learn well and work well, and contribute to their community."[50]

Mental Illness - a cluster of symptoms consistent with a diagnosable mental health condition which impacts a person's well-being and ability to function.

Neuroplasticity - the ability of the brain to adapt and change both in structure and function.

Neurotransmitter - a chemical messenger in the brain.

Noticing - giving attention to behavior without judgment.

Overvaluation - repeatedly assigning an undeserved high value to your child's character or behavior.

Perfect kid - a wonderful child whom you love who still has potential to develop a problem with substance use.

Pop Psychology - generic advice promoted in mainstream media or social media from professionals and lay people that is not tailored to individual circumstances.

Prefrontal Cortex - "This brain region has been implicated in executive functions, such as planning, decision making, short-term memory, personality expression, moderating social behavior and controlling certain aspects of speech and language."[51]

Protective Factor - individual or environmental characteristics, conditions, or behaviors that reduce the effects of stressful life events.

Psychoactive substance - a chemical that, when received by the brain, causes a change in the way the brain functions.

Psychotic symptoms - includes delusions (false beliefs) or hallucinations (seeing or hearing things that others do not see or hear) that cause a disconnection from reality.[52]

Restorative - allowing an opportunity to repair harm and restore connection.

Risk Factor - individual or environmental characteristics, conditions or behaviors that increase the likelihood of developing problematic substance use.

Schema - "mental structures that an individual uses to organize knowledge and guide cognitive processes and behaviour. People use schemata (the plural of schema) to categorize objects and events based on common elements and characteristics and thus interpret and predict the world. New information is processed according to how it fits into these mental structures, or rules."[53]

Scare tactics - messaging that aims to shock or frighten someone.

Schizophrenia - mental illness that may include symptoms of delusions, hallucinations and disorganized speech and/or behavior causing disconnection from reality.

Social and emotional learning (SEL) – developing knowledge, skills and attitudes for healthy sense of identity, coping with emotions, relating to others and making healthy decisions.

Teachable moments - situations that present an opportunity to share information, making it relevant and tangible.

Toxic shame - internalized shame that negatively impacts a person's sense of self-worth.

Trauma - an event that threatens someone's physical safety or bodily integrity or the safety of a loved one. "Traumatic experiences can initiate strong emotions and physical reactions that can persist long after the event."[54]

NOTES

[1] "Why You Should Talk with Your Child about Alcohol and Other Drugs." SAMHSA, Substance Abuse and Mental Health Services Administration, https://www.samhsa.gov/talk-they-hear-you/parent-resources/why-you-should-talk-your-child.

[2] "Using Fear Messages and Scare Tactics in Substance Abuse Prevention Efforts." Substance Abuse and Mental Health Services Administration, 30 Nov. 2015.

[3] "What Every Parent and Caregiver Needs to Know about Fake Pills." Dea.gov, Drug Enforcement Administration, Sept. 2022, https://www.dea.gov/sites/default/files/2022-11/DEA-OPCK_Parent%20flyer_V6.pdf.

[4] "Teens." Centers for Disease Control and Prevention, Centers for Disease Control and Prevention, 8 Sept. 2021, https://www.cdc.gov/marijuana/health-effects/teens.html.

[5] NIDA. "Genetics and Epigenetics of Addiction DrugFacts." National Institute on Drug Abuse, 5 Aug. 2019, https://nida.nih.gov/publications/drugfacts/genetics-epigenetics-addiction Accessed 21 Dec. 2021.

[6] NIDA. "Genetics and Epigenetics of Addiction DrugFacts." National Institute on Drug Abuse, 5 Aug. 2019, https://nida.nih.gov/publications/drugfacts/genetics-epigenetics-addiction Accessed 21 Dec. 2021.

[7] Patel, Shweta et al. "The Association Between Cannabis Use and Schizophrenia: Causative or Curative? A Systematic Review." Cureus vol. 12,7 e9309. 21 Jul. 2020, doi:10.7759/cureus.9309

[8] Maria Mavrikaki, PhD, Harvard Health Blog. https://www.health.harvard.edu/blog/your-genes-and-addiction-2019012815730 January 28, 2019.

[9] Lortye, S.A., Will, J.P., Marquenie, L.A. et al. Treating posttraumatic stress disorder in substance use disorder patients with co-occurring posttraumatic stress disorder: study protocol for a randomized controlled trial to compare the effectiveness of different types and timings of treatment. BMC Psychiatry 21, 442 (2021). https://doi.org/10.1186/s12888-021-03366-0.

[10] . "Making the Connection: Trauma and Substance Abuse." The National Child Traumatic Stress Network, June 2008.

[11] Genomind. "3 Things Genetic Testing Can Tell Us about Addiction." Genomind, 15 Apr. 2020, https://www.genomind.com/blog/addiction-genetic-testing-tell-us-substance-abuse.

[12] Abrams, Z. (2022, August 25). What neuroscience tells us about the teenage brain. Monitor on Psychology, 53(5). https://www.apa.org/monitor/2022/07/feature-neuroscience-teen-brain.

[13] GSD 2016 Alcohol Collaborators. "Alcohol Use and Burden for 195 Countries and Territories, 1990–2016: a Systematic Analysis for the Global Burden of Disease Study 2016." The Lancet, vol. 392, no. 10152, 23 Aug. 2018, pp. 1015–1035., https://pubmed.ncbi.nlm.nih.gov/30146330/.

[14] Shinkman, Paul D. "Study: No Amount of Alcohol Is Healthy - US News & World Report." US News & World Report, US News & World Report, 23 Aug. 2018, https://www.usnews.com/news/best-countries/articles/2018-08-23/study-assessment-of-drinkers-worldwide-shows-no-amount-of-alcohol-is-healthy.

[15] "Early Drinking Linked to Higher Lifetime Alcoholism Risk." National Institute on Alcohol Abuse and Alcoholism, U.S. Department of Health and Human Services, 3 July 2006, https://www.niaaa.nih.gov/news-events/news-releases/early-drinking-linked-higher-lifetime-alcoholism-risk.

[16] "Substance Use and Suds in LGBTQ* Populations." National Institutes of Health, U.S. Department of Health and Human Services, 3 June 2022, https://nida.nih.gov/research-topics/substance-use-suds-in-lgbtq-populations.

[17] "Substance Use and Suicide Risk among LGBTQ Youth." The Trevor Project, The Trevor Project, 27 Jan. 2022, https://www.thetrevorproject.org/research-briefs/substance-use-and-suicide-risk-among-lgbtq-youth-jan-2022/.

[18] "Substance Use and Suicide Risk among LGBTQ Youth." The Trevor Project, The Trevor Project, 27 Jan. 2022, https://www.thetrevorproject.org/research-briefs/substance-use-and-suicide-risk-among-lgbtq-youth-jan-2022/.

[19] Lynskey, M. T., & Agrawal, A. (2018). Denise Kandel's classic work on the gateway sequence of drug acquisition. Addiction (Abingdon, England), 113(10), 1927–1932. https://doi.org/10.1111/add.14190.

[20] Ren, M., & Lotfipour, S. (2019). Nicotine Gateway Effects on Adolescent Substance Use. The western journal of emergency medicine, 20(5), 696–709. https://doi.org/10.5811/westjem.2019.7.41661

[21] Raypole, Crystal. "Dopamine Addiction: A Guide to Dopamine's Role in Addiction." Healthline, Healthline Media, 30 Apr. 2019, https://www.healthline.com/health/dopamine-addiction.

[22] Raypole, Crystal. "Dopamine Addiction: A Guide to Dopamine's Role in Addiction." Healthline, Healthline Media, 30 Apr. 2019, https://www.healthline.com/health/dopamine-addiction.

[23] "About Mental Health." Centers for Disease Control and Prevention, Centers for Disease Control and Prevention, 28 June 2021, https://www.cdc.gov/mentalhealth/learn/index.

htm.

24 "High Risk Substance Use in Youth." Centers for Disease Control and Prevention, Centers for Disease Control and Prevention, 29 Sept. 2022, https://www.cdc.gov/healthyyouth/substance-use/index.htm.

25 "Risk and Protective Factors - SAMHSA." Samhsa.gov, Substance Abuse and Mental Health Services Administration, https://www.samhsa.gov/sites/default/files/20190718-samhsa-risk-protective-factors.pdf.

26 "School Connectedness Helps Students Thrive." Centers for Disease Control and Prevention, Centers for Disease Control and Prevention, 28 Sept. 2022, https://www.cdc.gov/healthyyouth/protective/youth-connectedness-important-protective-factor-for-health-well-being.htm.

27 Hari, Johann. "Everything you think you know about addiction is wrong." TED, July 2015, https://www.ted.com/talks/johann_hari_everything_you_think_you_know_about_addiction_is_wrong.

28 "Monitoring Your Teen's Activities: What Parents and Families Should Know." Centers for Disease Control and Prevention, Centers for Disease Control and Prevention, 21 Nov. 2019, https://www.cdc.gov/healthyyouth/protective/factsheets/parental_monitoring_factsheet.htm.

29 Hogg, Tracy. Secrets of the Baby Whisperer: How to Calm, Connect, and Communicate with Your Baby. Ballantine Books, Jan 29, 2002.

30 Berman, Robby. "Teen Mental Health: CDC Data Reveal the Pandemic's Impact." Medical News Today, MediLexicon International, 12 Apr. 2022, https://www.medicalnewstoday.com/articles/teen-mental-health-in-the-pandemic-cdc-data-echo-a-cry-for-help.

31 Thompson, Derek. "Why American Teens Are so Sad." The Atlantic, Atlantic Media Company, 25 May 2022, https://www.theatlantic.com/newsletters/archive/2022/04/american-teens-sadness-depression-anxiety/629524/.

32 Siegel, Daniel J. And Tina Payne Bryson. The Whole-Brain Child: 12 Revolutionary Strategies to Nurture Your Child's Developing Mind. Langara College, 2016.

33 "5 Tips for Cultivating Empathy." Making Caring Common Project, Harvard Graduate School of Education, Mar. 2021, https://mcc.gse.harvard.edu/resources-for-families/5-tips-cultivating-empathy.

34 "About CDC." Centers for Disease Control and Prevention, Centers for Disease Control and Prevention, 31 Aug. 2022, https://www.cdc.gov/about/.

35 "Who We Are." SAMHSA, https://www.samhsa.gov/about-us/who-we-are.

36 Winfrey, Oprah. "Atlas of the Heart - Part 2." Oprah's Super Soul, Episode 362, Simplecast, December 1, 2021, https://podcasts.apple.com/us/podcast/oprahs-super-soul/id1264843400

[37] Aslanian, Anna. "How to Deal with Shame." The Gottman Institute, The Gottman Institute, 28 Oct. 2021, https://www.gottman.com/blog/how-to-deal-with-shame/.

[38] Brown Brené. Rising Strong: How the Ability to Reset Transforms the Way We Live, Love, Parent, and Lead. Random House Inc, 2017.

[39] Aslanian, Anna. "How to Deal with Shame." The Gottman Institute, The Gottman Institute, 28 Oct. 2021, https://www.gottman.com/blog/how-to-deal-with-shame/.

[40] Brummelman, Eddie. "Origins of Narcissism in Children." Proceedings of the National Academy of Sciences, vol. 112, no. 12, 12 Feb. 2015, pp. 3659–3662., https://www.pnas.org/doi/epdf/10.1073/pnas.1420870112.

[41] Sorensen, Michael S. "Use 'and' Instead of 'but' for More Effective Communication." Michael S. Sorensen, 5 June 2019, https://michaelssorensen.com/use-and-instead-of-but-for-more-effective-communication/.

[42] Håkansson, A., & Jesionowska, V. (2018). Associations between substance use and type of crime in prisoners with substance use problems - a focus on violence and fatal violence. Substance abuse and rehabilitation, 9, 1–9. https://doi.org/10.2147/SAR.S143251.

[43] Shahid, M., & Zeng, Q. (2011). Early detection of illicit drug use in teenagers. Innovations in clinical neuroscience, 8(12), 24–28.

[44] Santos-Longhurst, Adrienne. "Mouth Swab Drug Test: What to Expect." Healthline, Healthline Media, 24 Jan. 2020, https://www.healthline.com/health/mouth-swab-drug-test#how-they-work.

[45] "Blood Drug Testing." Labcorp, Labcorp, https://www.labcorp.com/organizations/employers/workplace-drug-testing/blood-drug-testing.

[46] Gryczynski J, Schwartz RP, Mitchell SG, O'Grady KE, Ondersma SJ, 2014. Hair drug testing results and self-reported drug use among primary care patients with moderate-risk illicit drug use. Drug Alcohol Depend. 141, 44–50. 10.1016/j.drugalcdep.2014.05.001.

[47] "What Is the Definition of Addiction?" American Society of Addiction Medicine, American Society of Addiction Medicine, 15 Sept. 2019, https://www.asam.org/quality-care/definition-of-addiction.

[48] Heshmat, Shahram. "What Is Confirmation Bias?" Psychology Today, Sussex Publishers, 23 Apr. 2015, https://www.psychologytoday.com/us/blog/science-choice/201504/what-is-confirmation-bias.

[49] Nielsen, David A et al. "Epigenetics of drug abuse: predisposition or response." Pharmacogenomics vol. 13,10 (2012): 1149-60. doi:10.2217/pgs.12.94.

[50] "Mental Health: Strengthening Our Response." World Health Organization, World Health Organization, 17 June 2022, https://www.who.int/en/news-room/fact-sheets/detail/mental-health-strengthening-our-response.

[51] "Prefrontal Cortex." Wikipedia, Wikimedia Foundation, 23 Nov. 2022, https://

en.m.wikipedia.org/wiki/Prefrontal_cortex.

52 "Understanding Psychosis." National Institute of Mental Health, U.S. Department of Health and Human Services, https://www.nimh.nih.gov/health/publications/understanding-psychosis.

53 Michalak, Katja. "schema". Encyclopedia Britannica, 3 Oct. 2019, https://www.britannica.com/science/schema-cognitive. Accessed 30 December 2021.

54 Peterson, Sarah. "About Child Trauma." The National Child Traumatic Stress Network, The National Child Traumatic Stress Network, 5 Nov. 2018, https://www.nctsn.org/what-is-child-trauma/about-child-trauma.